DETHRONING
MALE HEADSHIP

SECOND EDITION

Shirley Taylor

Shirley Taylor
www.shirleytaylor.net

Book Layout ©2015 BookDesignTemplates.com
Cover Art: Joan Delight Gordon

Dethroning Male Headship Copyright © Shirley Taylor 2013
Published by One Way Press, Orlando, Florida, 2013
Library of Congress Control Number: 2013930782

Dethroning Male Headship/Shirley Taylor. —2nd ed.
ISBN -13: 978-1517047160
ISBN-10: 1517047161

Jesus is our standard, and since Jesus did not commit women to husbands, or to males, and because Jesus did not deny women anything based on their being women, then we cannot in good stewardship of the gospel, do so either.

— SHIRLEY TAYLOR

Books by Shirley Taylor

Dethroning Male Headship: Second Edition

Women Equal – No Buts: Create in us a new song of equality

Women Equal – No Buts: Powered by the same Source

Outside the pastor's door: Reflections of a church secretary

Dethroning Male Headship (First Edition)

This book is dedicated to my husband Don who has been by my side in this journey of faith. He is my strongest supporter, and it was he who opened my eyes to the injustice of how women are treated by churches that will not allow women full expression of their faith through service.

Contents

A Word from the Author

"You're Shirley Taylor?" I was attending a Christians for Biblical Equality conference in Los Angeles, July 25, 2015, exactly five years after I had demanded an apology from the Council on Biblical Manhood and Womanhood in Orlando, Florida. "Yes, I am," I replied. She then said, "I saw your book *Dethroning Male Headship* just now. I wanted you to know that I bought your book a few months ago for a paper that I had to write in seminary."

Much has happened in the five years since I made the apology demand at the Seneca Falls 2 Christian Women's Conference, but one thing has not changed. Women have not won the right in fundamental Christian churches to be pastors or equals in their own homes.

Because this struggle continues, and because I have made a full commitment to do my part, it was time to release this updated and revised *Dethroning Male Headship, Second Edition.*

INTRODUCTION

Some things are so wrong and damage so many people that Christians must speak out against them. The Danvers Statement[1] is one of those things. If you are a Christian, with the exception of a few denominations, more than likely your church agrees with this Statement that says men are to be leaders of women and that only men can be leaders in the church.

The Bible does not say that, but the Danvers Statement does.

The Danvers Statement on Biblical Manhood and Womanhood was issued by the Council on Biblical Manhood and Womanhood (CBMW) as their charter statement in 1987 and was finalized a year later. This group is comprised of several denominations which bedded Southern Baptists with fundamental Presbyterians, Sovereign Grace Ministries, and Evangelical Free Church of America, just to name a few. They are headquartered in the Southern Baptist Theological Seminary in South Carolina, where one of their founders, Bruce Ware, is a professor of Christian Theology.

In 1991, the Danvers Statement was included in *Recovering Biblical Manhood and Womanhood: A Response to Evangelical Feminism*. This book is a collection of essays by various authors extolling male headship. It was compiled and edited by CBMW founders, Wayne Grudem and John Piper. It is still a best seller among evangelical Christians. My personal observation is that it is a book of the highest misogynistic views by Christian leaders today.

The Danvers Statement was made available to Christians with these words: *"We offer this statement to the evangelical world, knowing that it will stimulate healthy discussion, hoping that it will gain widespread assent."*

It did gain widespread assent. But widespread assent does not make it right. Down through the centuries, many have misinterpreted the Bible. Numerous religious practices and theologies have been proposed and have gained much assent until someone finally spoke up and pointed out the flaws and how they distorted Christianity. Protestants know this better than most, as they protested a 1,500 year tradition of religious practice.

It is my belief that this document, which many evangelical fundamental Christian churches and groups have accepted, is the reason Christian women have not been able to break through church culture and restrictions in order to answer God's call in their lives. It is because of this document that has found acceptance in seminaries and churches, that women cannot be ministers of the gospel or pastors, and are even denied equality in their own homes.

The Danvers Statement Affirmation #5 is the heart of the document, which is male headship. Affirmation #5 says: *"The Old Testament, as well as the New Testament, manifests the equally high value and dignity which God attached to the roles of both men and women (Genesis 1:26-27, 2:1; Galatians 3:28). Both Old and New Testaments also affirm the principle of male headship in the family and in the covenant community."*

Those who teach that male headship is a hindrance to Christianity and to families do not deny or gloss over the cultural fact of male headship in the Old and the New Testaments. However, we cannot find a spiritual reason to continue that patriarchal familial and societal relationship in the 21st century. Nor can we find a spiritual reason to continue male headship in church leadership.

It is critical that Christians understand where this modern day claim of male headship came from. Christians must understand who wrote the Danvers Statement and also those who continue to promote it through various denominational faith statements and teachings in individual churches.

Forerunner of Baptist Faith and Message 2000

The Southern Baptist Convention (SBC) revised their Baptist Faith and Message 1963 and made it a document patterned after the Danvers Statement. This became the Baptist Faith and Message 2000 (BF&M2000). Since many of those who wrote the Danvers Statement were Southern Baptists, this was a progressive step designed to change every SBC church and organizational entity affiliated with the Southern Baptist Convention. From that time onward, the official statement of the SBC would embrace male headship.

Although Baptist entities and organizations are fully autonomous, they choose to be guided by the precepts of the national organization which is the Southern Baptist Convention, and most have chosen to follow the Baptist Faith and Message 2000.

Women are excluded from full service to God by the section in the BF&M2000 called The Church: "While both men and women are gifted for service in the church, the office of pastor is limited to men as qualified by Scripture." While that section eliminates women from pastoral or preaching ministries, it is the Section on the Family that was inserted into the newly rewritten Baptist Faith and Message 2000 that should concern all women:

> "A wife is to submit herself graciously to the servant leadership of her husband even as the church willingly submits to the headship of Christ. She, being in the image of God as is her husband and thus equal to him, has the God-given responsibility to respect her husband and to serve as his helper in managing the household and nurturing the next generation."

So now, these two, the Danvers Statement, along with the new Baptist Faith and Message 2000,[2] bestowed upon men an authority they called "headship" which would be over all Christian women within their homes and churches. This is known as *male headship*. Both documents state that women cannot be pastors, and that women must submit to the leadership of their husbands. When a church or seminary affirms either statement, it is specifically these two principles they are endorsing.

While the term "male headship" is not recognized in some Christian denominations that have chosen to allow women pastors and lay leaders, it is, nevertheless, the term used in fundamental churches.

The softer expression sometimes used is 'male *leadership*' which does not have the sweeping, encompassing meaning that 'male *headship*' does. In the pages of this book, we will learn how the Bible dethrones male headship and how we can work toward equality of women and men in the church and home.

Egalitarian versus Complementarian

Among Christians, there are two generally accepted views on how women are to be treated in the church and also in the home. Each view has variations as some adherents are more restrictive than others. The majority of people have never considered themselves to be either complementarian or egalitarian. However, whichever teaching a church, or denomination, or individual subscribes to, one of those terms will apply.

Egalitarian means that men and women are created equal—no buts—and as such, have no assigned roles of authority or submission based on gender. Women can answer God's call to preach, can pastor churches, and can be deacons and elders in churches. Women are equal in their homes with both husbands and wives submitting to each other.

Egalitarian is the view I believe and advocate for.

Complementarian is a word coined by the writers of the Danvers Statement to describe their teaching which they believe sets the guidelines for how men and women best complete or complement each other. It means that men and women have certain roles which, they claim, define manhood and womanhood. A man's role is to have authority over his wife and to have authority in the church. A woman's role is to be submissive to and supportive of her husband. She must follow her husband's leadership in everything. Because of this teaching about the family, women cannot have authority over men in church.

Some complementarians insist that women are to refrain from assuming authority over men even in the workplace. The wife's "role" of submission is praised and glorified. She is told that she is equal—but. Equal, but according to something they call *God's grand design*, she is to have a lesser position in the church, in her own home, and even before her children. Men and women who are unmarried must also adhere to the roles prescribed for their gender: leadership and authority for males and submissiveness for females.

This teaching keeps all women in a permanent subordinate position.

This book is a call to action

In the year 2000, while employed by the Baptist General Convention of Texas, I became convinced that the Southern Baptist Convention was starting down a path of returning women to the confines of patriarchy. The Southern Baptist Convention, which is the largest grouping of Protestants, decided that women should be frozen in time with archaic first century restrictions placed on them via "roles" they can or cannot fulfill within their homes and churches, while men, on the other hand, have been permitted to move into the 21st century with no restrictions at all.

On July 24, 2010, at the Seneca Falls 2 Christian Women's Conference in Orlando, Florida, this writer, and eight others, protested by demanding an apology from the Council on Biblical Manhood and Womanhood (CBMW) for their teaching of male headship that denigrates women. You will find the list of concerns and demands in Part 3 of this book. The Danvers Statement and my comments on what this document really means can be found in Part 2 of this book.

There are numerous types of Baptists but I have chosen to use Baptists and Southern Baptists as synonymous terms. The Southern Baptist Convention is not a denomination but is commonly referred to as a denomination. With their adoption of the Baptist Faith and Message 2000, many Baptists are concerned that the SBC is now functioning as a denomination.

This book is a call to action based upon an understanding that the scriptures teach that men and women are equal. Women were created equal with men by God, the Creator. While churches, Christianity, and society, have lost sight of that equality, women have always been equal in the mind of God. Women are reclaiming that equality.

Throughout this work, the "Danvers Statement on Biblical Manhood and Womanhood" will be discussed and referred to just as the "Danvers Statement."

So, with a bit of laughter, because we must laugh, and a lot of righteous indignation, it is hoped that the reader will have a clearer understanding of this terrible muddle of restrictions against women, and what we must do to get out of it. Our business as Christians is not to oppress women in order to elevate men. It is to elevate Christ in order that others may see Him through us.

Above all, the explanation will be kept simple.

PART 1

THE BIBLE DETHRONES MALE HEADSHIP

Fear the Lord your God, serve him only and take your oaths in his name. Do not follow other gods, the gods of the peoples around you; for the Lord your God, who is among you, is a jealous God and his anger will burn against you, and he will destroy you from the face of the land.

Deuteronomy 6:13

CHAPTER 1

In the beginning

In the beginning God made man and woman in his image. He made man to rule over animals—not over his wife.

Where did I come from? These are words that in times past would strike fear in the heart of every mother when her young child asked that question. We no longer tell our children that the stork brought them or that they came from the cabbage patch. But even in this enlightened age, there are some things about sexuality and reproduction that small children cannot understand, and they cannot grasp the meaning of the words used to tell the facts of their conception and birth.

Ancient people wanted to know the answer to that age-old question of where did we come from. Like a small child who would not understand the whole answer, we are given the beautiful story of creation in Genesis. We trace our lineage and understanding of God back to Adam and Eve. While we do not know the whole story, there are certain truths in the original story upon which we build our faith.

The first creation story, found in Genesis 1:26-31, says, "Then God said, Let us make man in our image, in our likeness, and let them rule over the fish of the sea and the birds of the air, over the livestock, over all the earth, and over all the creatures that move along the ground. So God created man in his own image, in the image of God he created him; male and female he created them."

In this first creation account, God did not give the man headship over the woman. To do so would have made her like the animals, the birds, and the plants of the earth. Instead, she, like the man, was made in God's image and was also commanded to rule over the animals, birds, and plants.

The second creation story

The Danvers Statement, explained in the Introduction of this book, uses the *second* Creation story found in the second chapter of Genesis. Their Affirmation #3 says: "Adam's headship in marriage was established by God before the Fall and was not a result of sin (Genesis 2:16-18, 21-24, 3:1-13, 1 Corinthians 11:7-9)." The Fall is when the snake persuaded Eve to eat the fruit of the tree of good and evil, then Eve gave the apple to Adam and he bit. She has been blamed for it ever since.

The scripture reference they give of Genesis 2:24 does not prove the point the Danvers Statement attempts to make in their Affirmation #3. This scripture says, "For this reason a man will leave his father and mother and be united to his wife, and they will become one flesh." That has nothing to do with headship as both husbands and wives are to leave their parents' home. Complementarians, who believe and teach that men are to rule over women, give "one flesh" a sexual meaning. The better explanation is that becoming one flesh indicates "oneness" or equality in the marriage. How the newly created Adam knew about marriage and mothers and fathers is another story.

This second creation story, the one complementarians prefer, depicts a lonely, naked Adam naming the bulls and cows as they came by. Looking down at his own body he must have seen that he was similar to a bull with male reproductive organs.

So the question arises, why did God suddenly decide Adam needed a mate? The answer is that God did not suddenly decide anything. Adam did not know it yet, but God already had a plan for him, because it was not good for this first man to be all alone. Before God made the bulls and the cows, human reproduction had already been patterned. Physically, there had to be a mate for Adam.

At no point do the Scriptures say that God created a mate for Adam to rule over. God gave Adam a companion who was equal to him, thus no headship was needed. And oh yes! he needed a mate so, together, they could produce a next generation. By himself, Adam was incomplete as he had only one-half the DNA required to make a baby. It would be many thousands of years before science revealed that Eve contributed the same amount of her DNA to their child. Had early humans had this knowledge, it should have changed forever the concept of women as unequal contributors in creating new generations.

Attempt to justify male headship

Trying to justify their theology of male headship, the Danvers Statement Affirmation #4 says: "*The Fall introduced distortions into the relationships between men and women* (Genesis 3:1-7, 12, 16)." Now let's get this straight. In Affirmation #1 they say "Both Adam and Eve were created in God's image, equal before God as persons and distinct in their manhood and womanhood (Genesis 1:26-27:2:18)."

Here they say that men and women were created equal, but they say Adam and Eve were *actually unequal* by the very fact that Adam was a male imbued with male superiority (distinct in their manhood), and by the fact that he was created first. Then Eve brought distortion into men and women's relationships by taking a bite of the apple before Adam bit into it. That does not make one bit of sense. It will not hold water. It is made-up theology. And neither do their scripture references back it up.

The reason it was so important in 1988 for the Danvers Statement to give Adam male headship before the Fall was that they had to establish that male headship could never be changed. However, since that time, the Eternal Son Subordination[1] teaching has been revived and has found favor, and, according to followers, justification, since they believe Adam's headship before the fall followed the same pattern.[2]

The Bible tells of instances where God changed his mind when people prayed or petitioned him. In Exodus 32:11-14, when God said he would destroy the Israelites, Moses made intercessory prayer for them, and God relented and changed his mind. God changed his mind again in Jonah 3:10, and did not destroy the Ninevites when they turned from their evil ways. A Gentile woman in Matthew 15:22-28, pestered Jesus and talked back to him pleading her case, and Jesus said that because of her great faith, her request would be granted.

By claiming that Adam was given male headship *before* the Fall, then no amount of prayer and pleading could change the situation since it was God's plan all along. They were sending a message to women that prayers will be ineffective because male headship, according to them, is the order of creation, despite the fact that nothing in the Bible confirms that the order of creation made males God's favorite human beings.

Are they afraid of what will happen when women pray for equality? However, to reclaim the equality given at creation, women *must* pray for deliverance from the female denigration that is taught in seminaries and practiced in churches and homes. Women must pray for mankind to change their minds, because it is mankind who is out of step with God.

Both Adam and Eve were sent from the garden. The Eves of this world have always worked beside their husbands, tilling soil, planting, harvesting, managing the animals, and providing the household's food. Women's labor, both in childbearing and child rearing, is necessary. Some women work at home tending the children and managing the household, while multitudes of women leave their homes each day to trade their skills for a salary, just as men do.

Adam's job was to work the garden and take care of it, (Genesis 2:15). Eve's job was to work alongside him, offering him companionship. This was the Garden of Eden, Paradise. So where, exactly, would you get the picture of Adam ruling over Eve? It was the garden he was to subdue, not his wife.

The order of creation does not give headship

A passage that is often quoted as a proof-text for male headship is 1 Timothy 2:13-15 which says, "For Adam was formed first, then Eve. And Adam was not the one deceived; it was the woman who was deceived and became a sinner. But women will be saved through childbearing, if they continue in faith, love and holiness with propriety."

One pastor, who apparently does not understand the story of Jesus, wrote, "The pain associated with childbirth was the punishment for the woman's sin, but the joy and privilege of child rearing delivers women from the stigma of that sin."

This interpretation does not make sense. It flies in the face of everything Christians believe. In the first place, Adam ate the apple, too. In the second place, anyone who starts preaching that the only requirement for women to be saved is to have babies and be good should be pulled from the pulpit and given a good talking to about salvation.

Women do not want that kind of salvation. Faith in Jesus Christ is required for both men and women.

God designed physiology; man assigned roles

Much has been written on Genesis 1:27, which says, "So God created man in his own image, in the image of God he created him; male and female he created them." Jocelyn Andersen, in her book *Woman this is WAR*[3] explains that "both male and female were created equal, equal in relation to God as well as equal in relation to one another—both in moral theory and in practical application." Andersen goes on to say "Differences between men and women can safely be acknowledged and appreciated without accepting the fallacy that those differences mandate that one gender be placed in 'divine authority' over the other."

Being made in the image of God leads to much speculation, and our human minds cannot know with certainty what that means. But whatever it means, it applies to men and to women equally. There is not one set of roles for men and another set for women. God's grand design was to create both men and women. God designed physiology; man assigned roles.

Male headship ate the apple

If Adam had been a male headship kind of guy, if God had told him to take authority, he would have knocked that apple out of Eve's hand, picked up a stick and killed that snake.

Alas! Male headship ate the apple.

Male headship is dethroned by God himself when he made male and female in His own image.

CHAPTER 2

They asked for Sarah first

God's messengers asked for Sarah first—*before* speaking to Abraham.

In Genesis 12:2, God said to Abraham, "I will make you into a great nation and I will bless you; I will make your name great, and you will be a blessing." In Genesis 18:9-10, God's messengers asked, "Where is your wife Sarah?" Abraham replied, "There, in the tent." Then the LORD said, "I will surely return to you about this time next year, and Sarah your wife will have a son."

It is important to note that the messengers asked where Sarah was *before* Abraham was told that God's plan was coming together and that he and Sarah were finally going to become parents. They knew Sarah was listening at the entrance to the tent, which was right behind Abraham, ensuring that she would hear every word the messengers said.

The great nation foretold to descend from Abraham depended upon his wife Sarah, making her as important as Abraham in the founding of Israel. If male headship was important, the messengers who appeared to Abraham would not have even considered Sarah.

Telling Abraham would have been enough.

Father Abraham!

In Genesis chapters 15-21, Abraham's family story reads like a soap opera. We learn that God has promised Abram heirs, so many that they would be as numerous as the stars in the sky (Genesis 15:5), yet year after year, Abram remained childless.

Believing that Sarah was infertile (they believed that infertility was always the woman's fault), this Patriarch gave in to her insistence that he sleep with Hagar so Sarah could give Abraham a baby through her handmaid. Scientific miracles today make it possible for a grandma to give birth to her own grandchild through artificial means. Sarah might have used something like that to get a child if she could have, but she did not have it then, so she used who she could. That was Hagar.

Abram got Hagar pregnant. Then Sarai (her name had not yet been changed to Sarah) got mad at Hagar for getting pregnant. Father Abram (his name had not yet been changed to Abraham) told Sarai that Hagar was her responsibility, and she could do what she wanted with her maid. Now remember, Hagar's child was his child, too. He did not seem to care what happened to the mother or to the child. So, hot-tempered Sarai sent Hagar out to fend for herself. An angel found her and told her to go back to Sarai, and submit to her mistress.

Then God had another conversation with Abram in which he changed his name to identify what he was going to become, a father of nations. Abram's name was changed to Abraham, and Sarai must now be called Sarah, for she was destined to become a mother of nations. God told him that his covenant would be established through Isaac, the son born to Sarah. Then Abraham put in a plea for Ishmael, his son by Hagar, and God told him Ishmael would also be blessed and become the father of a great nation.

Let's look again at the day when the three men from the Lord appeared to Abraham as he sat by the door of his tent. He's old, she's old, a lot of promises had been made to Abraham, and it was now time he heard how it was all going to come about. Abraham made the messengers comfortable. He fed them, and then it was time to get down to business. But first, they asked, "Where is Sarah your wife?" They knew she was in the tent before they even asked and that she would be able to hear every word they said. They wanted her to know that they were sent to give this promise to her also.

A year later, Sarah birthed baby Isaac. Henceforth, she has become known as the Mother of Israel.

Abraham's story dethrones male headship

Look at the definition of male headship as defined in the Danvers Statement. Affirmation #6 says, "In the family, husbands should forsake harsh or selfish leadership and grow in love and care for their wives; wives should forsake resistance to their husbands' authority and grow in willing, joyful, submission to their husbands' leadership."

With hotheaded Sarah sending Hagar out to starve—twice— Abraham was *not* lovin' his family. The first time Sarah became angry with Hagar, Abraham told Sarah to do what she wanted with her. He did not care. The second time, after he had become fond of Ishmael, Abraham protested but was told by God to follow *Sarah's leadership* in this instance.

God said "Listen to whatever Sarah tells you, because it is through Isaac that your offspring will be reckoned." God encouraged Abraham to obey this command by promising, "I will make the son of the maidservant into a nation also, because he is your offspring."

With regard to this situation, Abraham's authority over Sarah was non-existent, because God was leading the women in the direction He chose, and He had an angel on standby waiting to help Hagar and Ishmael after they were banished to the desert (Genesis 21:12-19).

The powerful message of 1 Peter 3:1-6

Some like to quote Peter when he said Sarah called Abraham "master" in Genesis 18:12, "So Sarah laughed to herself as she thought, 'After I am worn out and my master is old, will I now have this pleasure?'" The New International Version Bible uses the word "master," unlike other translations that use the word "Lord."

It is impossible to connect 1 Peter 3:1-6 to the words of Sarah found in Genesis to support the doctrine of wifely submission, but Bruce Ware, one of the founding members of the Council on Biblical Manhood and Womanhood, attempts to do just that in his book, *The*

Father, the Son, and the Holy Spirit: The Trinity as Theological Foundation for Family Ministry.[1]

Ware writes, "I find it astonishing that it is in this text, of all New Testament passages that teach on husband and wife relations, that the strongest language is used to describe a wife's submission! Peter appealed to Sarah as an example and said that she "obeyed Abraham, calling him lord" (1 Pet 3:6a), indicating that they would be Sarah's "children" if they fearlessly followed this example."

Ware, who is a professor of Christian Theology, has missed the beautiful promise of this passage. The promise is not that women would be Sarah's *children* if they are submissive, but that they would become *mothers* like Sarah because they themselves would be founding a new nation of believers, not by giving birth in the physical sense, but by spreading the gospel message so people can be born *again* by the spirit.

To emphasize, Peter does NOT tell wives they are Sarah's daughters if they submit to their husbands like Sarah did. What he DOES say was startling, and likely raised the hairs on their heads by its audacity. Peter tells these women that "like mother, like daughter" and just as their mother Sarah birthed a new nation, they, too, are birthing a new nation of believers.

We can interpret Peter's words something like this, "That was the way it was done back in Sarah's day, but things have changed. We are now under grace by faith, not under the law. You have done what is right in becoming Christ-followers, and are Sarah's daughters—children of the freed woman—if you do not fear as you keep following Christ, and, like Sarah, *you will birth* this new nation of God's people."

Again, Paul says the same thing:

"Tell me, you who want to be under the law, are you not aware of what the law says? For it is written that Abraham had two sons, one by the slave woman and the other by the free woman. His son by the slave woman was born in the ordinary way, but his son by the free woman was born as the result of a promise. These things may be taken figuratively, for the women represent two covenants. One covenant is from Mount Sinai and bears children who are to be slaves: This is Hagar. Now Hagar stands for Mount Sinai in Arabia and corresponds to the present city of Jerusalem, because she is in slavery with her children. But the Jerusalem that is above is free, and she is our mother (Sarah)....Therefore, brothers, we are not children of the slave woman, but of the free woman" (Galatians 4:21-26, 31).

Mothers of a nation of believers!

1 Peter 3 contains a powerful promise of building a nation of believers that is for all time.

Twenty-first century Christian women are also children of the free woman, but some still choose to cling to Hagar by holding to a master/slave relationship with their husbands, and pastors still enforce this type of submission, even when they know it is wrong.

Sarah is mentioned four times in the New Testament, three of which are specifically about her becoming the mother of a nation. 1 Peter 3:6 is too, but the greater truth of it has been neglected. By passionately claiming the first part of the scripture that says wives must submit to their husbands, the promise it held for New Testament wives has been ignored. This particular reference to Sarah in 1 Peter 3:6 emphasizes the new covenant and has those new Christian women actively participating in the ministry of the gospel by birthing a nation of believers (1 Peter 3:6; Hebrews 11:11; Romans 4:19; Galatians 4:2-26, 31).

Wives, continue in your marriages even if your husbands are unbelievers, for by doing so, you will be like Sarah, *mothers* of a nation of believers.

Male headship is dethroned when Peter told Christian women that they will be like Sarah, mothers of a nation of believers.

CHAPTER 3

No commandment for male headship

When Jesus was asked "which is the greatest commandment in the Law?" He replied, "Love the Lord your God with all your heart and with all your soul and with all your mind. This is the first and greatest commandment. And the second is like it: Love your neighbor as yourself. All the Law and the Prophets hang on these two commandments" (Matthew 22:36-40).

If male headship was so important, Jesus would have mentioned it, and it would have been included in the Ten Commandments and the 5ᵗʰ Command would have read something like this:

1. You shall have no other gods before me
2. You shall not make for yourself an idol
3. You shall not make wrongful use of the name of your God
4. Remember the Sabbath and keep it holy
5. Honor your father as head of the family *(instead of honor your father and mother)*
6. You shall not murder
7. You shall not commit adultery
8. You shall not steal
9. You shall not bear false witness against your neighbor
10. You shall not covet your neighbor's wife nor anything that belongs to your neighbor

God Himself dethroned male headship by not making it one of the Ten Commandments

It is very telling that God did not include male headship in the Ten Commandments. It deals with such things as lying, stealing, murdering, committing adultery, and desiring what your neighbor owns. In the one place where we would expect to find the husband commanded to lead his family, we find, instead, a commandment to honor *both* mother and father. The 5th Commandment signifies *equality* in marriage by giving mothers equal honor with fathers.

Jesus also lays the foundation for equality with his summation of the Ten Commandments. "Love your neighbor as yourself" suggests equality; equality with other races, to be sure, but also equality of the sexes.

The 10th Commandment is the only commandment directed specifically toward males. It is found in Exodus 20:17 and says, "Do not covet your neighbor's house. Do not covet your neighbor's wife, his male or female slave, his ox or donkey, or anything that belongs to your neighbor."

The 10th Commandment lumps women in with the donkeys and household belongings. Some egalitarians believe that this is due to the patriarchal society in which it was written, but there is possibly a different interpretation that has been missed. Look at it this way. Imagine God is talking to a man. He tells the man that just because he is a man, he cannot look over into his neighbor's yard and start picking out the things he wants. The neighbor's wife and his male and female servants are not his to take (remember King David broke this commandment). Suppose this commandment actually diminishes the exalted idea a man might have of himself. It brings his ideas of male headship down to earth. It prohibits wife-swapping and wife stealing. It also prohibits using male and female servants as sex slaves. It is the only commandment directed specifically towards men, and it certainly does not bestow upon them male headship.

If male headship is a biblical commandment and as important as the Danvers Statement says it is, and as critical as the Baptist Faith and Message 2000 Section on the Family indicates, then why did Jesus neglect to work it into the greatest Commandments when he was asked which commandments were the most important? Surely they would have needed to know this also.

The Danvers Statement states that women who claim equality with men are destroying the fabric of society, Concern #10. According to the Council on Biblical Manhood and Womanhood, the only thing that will save society is for men to dominate women by "reclaiming" male headship.

If all society hinges on what a woman does or does not do, and on what she is allowed or not allowed to do, then Jesus would certainly have said so. It would have been as important as loving God and your neighbor. Instead, he said that all the Law and the Prophets hang on loving God and loving your neighbor as yourself. And in these words, male headship is nowhere to be found.

Male headship is dethroned because it is not in the Commandments, nor is it in the words of Jesus.

CHAPTER 4

Mary makes a decision

The angel Gabriel was sent to announce two upcoming births. First he went to Zechariah to tell him that his wife Elizabeth would give birth to a son. That son would be John the Baptizer. Zechariah was surprised when the angel appeared to him, and he asked, "How can I be sure of this? I am an old man, and my wife is well along in years." The angel answered, "I am Gabriel. I stand in the presence of God, and I have been sent to speak to you and to tell you this good news" (Luke 1:18-19).

After that, the angel Gabriel did something very unusual. He went *directly to Mary*, who would become the mother of Jesus, to announce the important news of this upcoming miraculous conception and birth.

In Luke 1:26-31, the greatest news of all time, the birth of Jesus, is announced to a *woman*. "In the sixth month, God sent the angel Gabriel to Nazareth, a town in Galilee, to a virgin pledged to be married to a man named Joseph, a descendant of David. The virgin's name was Mary. The angel went to her and said, 'Greetings, you who are highly favored! The Lord is with you.'

Mary was greatly troubled at his words and wondered what kind of greeting this might be. But the angel said to her, 'Do not be afraid, Mary, you have found favor with God. You will be with child and give birth to a son, and you are to give him the name Jesus.' 'How will this be,' Mary asked the angel, 'since I am a virgin?'"

It is certain that this young girl had never made an important decision apart from her family in all her life. The culture she lived in guaranteed that. The angel's announcement required an independent decision on her part. First, she wrestled with the greeting. She questioned how she, a young girl who was a virgin, could give birth to a baby. Gabriel had to convince her. At the end of their conversation she agreed to cooperate with God's plan. It was after that acceptance that the angel went to Joseph to tell him what was going to happen.

Mary decides

That was in direct contrast to the angels' announcement to Sarah and Abraham. When Sarah was told by the messengers that she would give birth to a son, she laughed but had no voice in the decision. Similarly, when Elizabeth was told by her husband that she would birth a son, it was already a done deal. But when Mary was told that God had found favor with her, and that she would miraculously conceive a child who would be the long-awaited Messiah, *she* was called upon to decide. She questioned, she listened, she considered, and then she made her decision, "I am the Lord's servant," Mary answered. "May it be to me as you have said."

An out of wedlock pregnancy could bring serious consequences upon Mary and her family. The man she was going to marry faced humiliation and could have had her stoned to death as an adulterous woman. Her father or Joseph most certainly would not have permitted the pregnancy before marriage—Messiah or no—had it been up to them. Mary could have deflected responsibility for the decision by telling the angel there was no way she could accept this honor without first asking permission of her father or Joseph, as this was far too significant a decision for a mere woman to make without male advice or permission. But she did not. The angel could have first gone to her father or to Joseph and told them what was going to happen to Mary, just like he had gone to Zechariah. But he did not.

Instead, the angel Gabriel went directly to a young *woman*, giving her the greatest news that all mankind would ever hear, and left the decision up to her whether or not to accept the honor and the awesome responsibility of becoming the mother of the Messiah.

Male headship is dethroned because God sent the angel Gabriel to a female, who made the decision by herself to accept the honor of becoming the mother of the Messiah.

CHAPTER 5

The woman at the well

The Danvers Statement Affirmation #9 says: "With half the world's population outside the reach of indigenous evangelism; with countless other lost people in those societies that have heard the gospel; with the stresses and miseries of sickness, malnutrition, homelessness, illiteracy, ignorance, aging, addiction, crime, incarceration, neuroses, and loneliness, no man or woman who feels a passion from God to make His grace known in word and deed need ever live without a fulfilling ministry for the glory of Christ and the good of this fallen world."

No matter what shape the world is in, the writers of the Danvers Statement would never have chosen the woman at the well to be the instrument God used to win people to Christ.

But Jesus did.

Everyone knows her story. In fact, hers is one of the longest detailed stories of an event in the New Testament. It was her story. She told it to everyone who would listen. This man she had just met at the well knew that she had had five husbands and was now living with a man who was not her husband.

Jesus was not judging her for that. He was offering her something that no man could offer a woman. He was offering her living water—from a well that would never run dry. And he told her that *he* was the source of this living water.

This was a woman experienced in the ways of men, and she knew this conversation was different from any she had ever had. She was certainly not the one who would be expected to announce the news that prophecy had been fulfilled and that the long-awaited Messiah had finally arrived for the Samaritans. No one would even listen to a *woman* proclaiming this momentous event, would they? But for some reason, Jesus chose her to reveal his true identity.

She took that message and ran with it.

It was Jesus who brought up the subject of living water. He told her that if she drank from the water he gave, she would never be thirsty again.

She wanted that. She said she did not want to keep coming to the well to draw water. She was probably teasing him at that point as she had no idea what he was talking about. Then Jesus did something surprising. He told her to go call her husband and then to come back.

Aha! Finally Jesus brings male headship into the conversation! "Go, call your husband and come back," Jesus said.

The woman answered, "I have no husband."

Was Jesus surprised at this? Did he ask her to go call her husband just to embarrass her? No, its significance is greater than her confession that she was not married to the man with whom she was living. She was worthy in her own right, as a woman, to be told *directly by him* that he was the Messiah.

They then engaged in a theological discussion. This woman was not learning in silence. And Jesus did not rebuke her for it. She talked back and told him that she could see that he was a prophet. She declared "I know that Messiah (called Christ) is coming. When he comes, he will explain everything to us."

And he did explain—right then and there—to the woman at the well, a woman who did not have a husband to tell her if what she was hearing was right or wrong. She heard, she accepted, she told.

Mission accomplished in Samaria

This story of the woman at the well is found in John 4:4-42 and begins by saying, "Now he had to go through Samaria." It is best translated that "he purposed in his mind" to go through Samaria, because the Jews had found a way, even though it was inconvenient, to avoid Samaria. They thought they were better than these poor cousins, the Samaritans, and for a Jew to deliberately go through Samaria was unusual.

There was something in Samaria that Jesus needed to do in order to complete his earthly work.

It appears that Jesus was covering the bases with women. Every message of importance was given to women:

- **Women could learn the scriptures**. The Jewish woman, Mary of Bethany, was welcomed by Jesus to sit at his feet right beside the men, and learn at a time when learning scripture was forbidden to women.
- **Gentiles would be in the kingdom**. The Gentile woman was told by Jesus that he was sent not only to Israel, but to all people, which included her.
- **The Messiah had come to the Samaritans.** The Samaritan woman received the news that he was the Messiah, whom the Samaritans were also expecting, since they claimed theirs was the true religion of the ancient Israelites.
- **The resurrection.** At the tomb, a *woman* would be the first to see and speak with the resurrected Jesus.

These are pivotal stories because they show that Jesus gives the voice of the gospel to women just as he gives the voice of the gospel to men. These stories also set the stage for the empty tomb where it was women who first encountered the resurrected Jesus and where the full gospel of the death and resurrection of Jesus would unfold. So, yes, Jesus *purposed in his mind* to go through Samaria, because he had something to complete in Samaria.

The completion of this mission was so satisfying to him that he told his disciples, "I have food to eat that you know nothing about." The conversation he had with this woman had an effect upon Jesus that was profoundly different from his other encounters with men or women. This is the only scripture passage in the Bible where Jesus said that what had just happened was so meaningful to him that he felt that he had been fed. In other words, mission accomplished.

Verse 42 says "...we no longer believe just because of what you said; now we have heard for ourselves, and we know that this man really is the Savior of the world." These men first heard the words of Jesus from a woman, and then they heard the same message from Jesus himself.

Male headship was dethroned and women elevated by Jesus when he said to the Samaritan woman "I, who speak to you, am he."

CHAPTER 6

The Good News preacher

"He is risen!" the shout was heard that first Easter morning. Even today Christians greet each other "He is risen!" and the response comes back "He is risen, indeed!"

That is the gospel.

In those simple words, the good news of the death and resurrection of Jesus Christ is expressed. According to the apostle Paul, that is the entirety of the gospel of Christ (1 Corinthians 15:3-5).

Those words were first conveyed by a *woman*.

There were surely men available who could have relayed this important news. There were male soldiers at the tomb. They were scared to death. Matthew 28:4 tells that they shook and became like dead men. If male headship had been bestowed on them at creation, it surely failed them that morning.

The facts come together in the four gospels where Matthew, Mark, Luke, and John tell different aspects of the same story. The scriptural witness is unanimous: it was women who first told the good news that Jesus had risen from the dead.

Matthew 28

Mary Magdalene and the other Mary saw an angel. The angel told the women not to be afraid for Jesus was risen. They left, and Jesus met them. The women took hold of his feet and worshipped him. Jesus told the women to *go tell* the men that he would meet them in Galilee.

Mark 16

Mary Magdalene and Mary the mother of James, and Salome saw the angel. The angel told them not to be afraid, that Jesus had risen. They left, trembled, and told no one. Mary Magdalene went to tell the disciples that he was alive and that she had seen Jesus. They did not believe her.

Luke 24

Women were told by the angel that Jesus was alive. Women told the disciples that he was risen. It was Mary Magdalene, Joanna, Mary the mother of James, and other women with them who went to the tomb with spices to anoint his dead body. They saw two angels in dazzling apparel. The angels told them that Jesus had risen. These women went to the disciples and told the eleven, and others, who did not believe them.

John 20

Jesus saw Peter and the other disciple at the tomb on resurrection morning, but did not appear to them. It was Mary to whom he revealed himself, "Mary," he said.

Mary Magdalene had gone to the tomb. She saw that the stone had been rolled away. She ran to tell Peter and the other disciple whom Jesus loved. These two men ran to the tomb. Jesus was not there, so they went back home.

But Mary stood weeping outside the tomb. Then she saw two angels (from the other gospel accounts we know that Mary was not the only woman there, but Mary is the only one John mentions). The angels told Mary that Jesus had risen. Mary saw Jesus but did not recognize him. He asked her why she wept. She told him she wept because they had taken away her Lord, and that she did not know where they had laid him. Then Jesus said, "Mary." And in that one word, he said everything. He then told her to go and tell the men. Mary went and told the disciples, "I have seen the Lord." And then she told them what he had said.

He is risen!

The angels did not speak to the men. Jesus did not appear to Peter and John. He deliberately saved the Good News for the women to hear and tell first.

It is hard to believe that Jesus gave this Good News to women if he intended to forbid them to preach the gospel, to restrict them to learn in silence, and limit them to teach only other women and children, and to forbid them to have an authoritative word in the church.

The 12 Disciples replaced by one woman!

Often those who are working for women's equality are asked why Jesus did not choose any women to be one of his disciples. The implication is that since Jesus chose only men, then it is only men Jesus wants to preach the gospel, or be a deacon or an elder. But look what happened! Jesus chose to tell one woman the Good News of his resurrection. Men were chosen before the cross, a woman was chosen after the cross.

Male headship was dethroned when Jesus told women, instead of the men who were there, that he had risen, and then he told the women to go and tell the men.

CHAPTER 7

Men *and* women persecuted

Saul (the Apostle Paul's name before his conversion) persecuted both men and women because they were followers of Jesus.

Paul would be shocked at the teaching today regarding the exalted status of males over females. He saw women as equally threatening to the Jewish law, so he persecuted both men *and women* because they followed the teaching of Jesus.

In Acts 8:1-3, with the martyrdom of Stephen, Saul began his tyranny against the church, "On that day a great persecution broke out against the church at Jerusalem, and all except the apostles were scattered throughout Judea and Samaria. Godly men buried Stephen and mourned deeply for him. But Saul began to destroy the church. Going from house to house, he dragged off men *and women* and put them in prison."

The story continues in Acts 9:1-2 where it says, "Meanwhile, Saul was still breathing out murderous threats against the Lord's disciples..." Saul began in Jerusalem, and in his zeal, he went from house to house dragging off men and women to be put into prison. He was not satisfied with just persecuting the Christians in Jerusalem, and he was not satisfied with persecuting just men. Saul wrote letters to the high priest and told him he was coming to Damascus and asked if the priest knew of anyone, man or woman, who was part of the Way, that he might take them as prisoners to Jerusalem.

Saul was determined to root out the Way people, the Christ follow-ers. He did not just talk about his plans. He put his words into action. He was determined to destroy the church.

Why did Saul drag defenseless women out of their beds in the middle of the night and take them off to prison? What harm were the-se women doing? If male headship had been in practice among these followers of Jesus, Saul would have known that all he had to do was take the men and put them prison.

If he cut off the heads, which were the men, then the women would not be threats, right?

But Saul knew better. He knew that the women of the Way experi-enced extraordinary freedom and were just as much a threat to his Jewish laws as the men were. He knew that the women who followed Jesus were vocal about their faith and were influencing others to fol-low Jesus as the men were. The zeal these women showed for their faith may be one of the reasons women later played such a large part in Paul's ministry.

Saul knew that among the people of the Way something had changed. And because of this change, he had to treat the men and women equally. He had to imprison and put to death both males and females who were followers of the Way.

> *Male headship was dethroned by Saul because he knew that he must stop both men and women from teaching the Way.*

God does not share headship with man

The apostle Paul did not teach that male headship was a biblical commandment (he told husbands to LOVE their wives as they love themselves).

Paul wrote for one purpose: to teach the death, burial, and resurrection of Jesus Christ and to edify the church. Outside of the message of Jesus, there was no message.

In 1 Corinthians 2:2, Paul wrote, "For I resolved to know nothing while I was with you except Jesus Christ and him crucified." In Chapter 3 verse 10, he wrote, "By the grace God has given me, I laid a foundation as an expert builder, and someone else is building on it. But each one should be careful how he builds. For no one can lay any foundation other than the one already laid, which is Jesus Christ."

This means others will add on to the basic gospel message with their own interpretations of who Jesus is. They will keep adding to the scriptures as if building a foundation, but they should be careful because there is only one foundation, and that is Jesus Christ. This is Paul's way of saying to keep the main thing, the main thing.

Complementarian teaching has added onto the foundation. They have made the foundation to be that of man and woman in a human marriage, of which more will be spoken about later in this book.

They have changed the definition of God. They have fashioned a human god by placing a husband between a woman and God. Because they emphasize that a wife is to submit to her husband, and that a husband is to take authority over his wife rather than husband and wife mutually submitting to each other, this makes the husband superior to God in the lives of many women. Complementarians insist that it does not. They ignore the fact that both men and women are to submit to God, and husbands and wives are to submit to each other equally.

Paul did not say God gave men headship over their wives, nor did he command husbands to rule over their wives. Paul used the marriage customs of his day to explain how Christ is the head of the church.

Man is not divine

1 Corinthians 11:3 says, "Now I want you to realize the head of every man is Christ, and the head of the woman is man, and the head of Christ is God."

Looking at that scripture, it is apparent something is wrong. But having heard the same explanation over and over, it is easy to fail to see what is right before our eyes.

- Christ is divine
- God is divine
- Christ is God is divine
- Man is *not* divine

A human man is out of context in a scripture about Christ being head of the church. Why was "the man is the head of the woman" inserted in the scripture? The complementarian interpretation of this scripture has husbands being inserted between a woman and God in the marriage ceremony. This scripture, taken at face value, makes the Trinity a Quartet.

No human has been divinely granted control over other humans; all are created in God's own image, equal, and who are also given dominion over all other creation. God did not make males divine. There is no scripture in the whole Bible that gives males divinity. Yet to fit into this scripture, all human men would have the potential to be divine. Divinity would be bestowed upon them when they married, giving them headship over their wives.

It did not fit. But why was it there?

It was put there because of Ephesians 5:12 where Paul says it is a profound mystery, but he is talking about Christ and the church, and the best way he knows how to relate it so they would understand, is to compare it to their own marriages. It was a favorite expression of Paul's, one he used time and again. Paul was not married and even said that it was preferable not to be married (1 Corinthians 7:1-7).

Interpret 1 Corinthians 11:3 this way "Now I want you to realize the head of every man and every woman is Christ (remember that I told you that it is like your own family where the husband is the head of the woman) and Christ has this authority because Christ has his beginning as God."

Then he gets into the long hair versus short hair, but since that argument is ignored in present day culture, it appears that modern day Christians are not to concern themselves with hair length. Paul was speaking to the men and women in the present tense—their present tense—their NOW, not in the past, and not in the future. He was saying, "This is the way it is right now." That is different from culture. Culture can go from the past to the present and into the future. It can change as time goes by, but the NOW is frozen in time with no past and no future.

Paul was neither establishing that husbands rightfully had headship over their wives, nor was he making it a condition for the future. He was simply saying that this is the way it is and he used that as an example to show them how Christ/God was the head of the church. Egalitarians do not deny that male dominated marriages were a fact of life in Paul's day; what egalitarians do deny is that a fact of life in a past culture becomes a biblical command to Christian women in the 21st century.

It is commonly taught that every scripture verse has a meaning for the time it was written and also for the future. But apparently it does not. If it did, pastors would tell women in their congregations that they dress like prostitutes and their clothing, makeup, and jewelry reflect badly upon Christ. Paul and Peter both wrote the same things with regard to how women were to dress in those same passages where they tell women to submit.

Complementarians cannot have it both ways

Complementarians cannot have it both ways. If women are to be held to part of the scriptures, then women should be held to all of it. If Paul was telling women how to dress in the future, then preachers are being derelict in their duties by not preaching against wearing jewelry, gold, and pearls. Church by-laws, the Baptist Faith and Message 2000, and the Danvers Statement should warn women about their attire in order to line up with scripture.

But they will not do that because they understand that culture has changed, and women in the 21st century who wear adornments are not looked upon as prostitutes. It is hard to understand how one part of a scripture passage can be attributed to culture while the other part is not.

Bob Allen, senior writer for Associated Baptist Press at the time, quoted Doug Phillips as he explains how difficult it is to apply certain cultural situations to people in the 21st century:

> "Doug Phillips, pastor of Oleander Church of God in Fort Pierce, Florida, said using selected passages written by Paul to prevent women from leadership in the church fails to distinguish between 'Paul's establishment of biblical principles' and specific cases that Paul dealt with that are 'lifted out of an antiquated social context.' Phillips said Paul's instructions to the church at Corinth—that women are to sit separately from men, dress modestly including covering their heads with veils and to learn in silence, were written in a society where men were accustomed to pagan fertility cults mediated by temple

prostitutes. 'We are totally divorced from that kind of historical and social context,' Phillips said. 'We have no idea what that means. You don't see him telling anybody else anywhere to cover up and wear veils and all that stuff. He was dealing with a special situation.' Phillips said it is 'just wrong' to apply social and cultural situations that are no longer relevant to the treatment of people in the 21st century."[1]

Phillips has an excellent point. It is wrong to "cherry pick" certain verses in order to apply irrelevant solutions and customs to women today, to attribute some to ancient culture, while others are credited as biblical commands against contemporary women.

Stay in the context of who you are

In 1 Peter 3:1, Peter instructed wives to be submissive to their husbands. He was essentially saying this, "Continue in your marriages as you have always done, submitting to your husbands. Do not divorce them because you are Christians now and they are not. It might be that you will have such an impact upon them that they become Christians when they see how you live." This scripture has a much deeper meaning as has been explained in Chapter 2 of this book "They asked for Sarah first."

When Peter goes on to talk about hair and clothes, he is continuing the same subject, which is to maintain a lifestyle that will successfully birth a new nation of believers rather than scaring others away from Christianity. Wearing fine clothing, gold, and pearls would set a woman apart as being wealthy, worldly, and above others. Therefore, Christian women were instructed to dress according to cultural norms so they would be seen as being inclusive and equal to those around them. They were to use their style of dress to promote equality, to become approachable so their husbands and others would feel free to ask questions, to discuss their choices, to consider aligning themselves with Christ. It was by eliminating social barriers, by avoiding radical change, and by staying in context of who they were before they became Christians, that they were more likely to attract others to Christ.

The same line of thought, which began with 1 Peter 2:13-21, is also found in 1 Corinthians 7:12-24, where it is expressed as staying in context with who you are. If you are married, stay married; if you are a slave, stay a slave; if you were circumcised when you were called, stay circumcised (it would be interesting to ask Paul to explain this one), if you were uncircumcised, then stay uncircumcised. It is all about being a Christian and still being who you are—as long as it is not sinful.

Quoting 1 Timothy 2:11-12 to silence women

Another scripture that is often used to keep women under control is 1 Timothy 2:9-15. Like the verses in 1 Peter and 1 Corinthians, this one also speaks about what a woman is to wear and begins with a dress code, "I also want women to dress modestly, with decency and propriety, not with braided hair or gold or pearls or expensive clothes."

Again, it is not how a woman dresses that complementarians use against women. It is verses 11-12 of that passage in 1 Timothy 2 that has become the main theological point, "A woman should learn in quietness and full submission. I do not permit a woman to teach or to have authority over a man; she must be silent."

These verses have been singled out because complementarians want to use them to silence women and to prohibit them from having authority over men. While there are some denominations and groups that insist upon a certain standard of dress for women, banning jewelry and determining certain hair styles for women, most do not. Most pastors ignore the part about the clothes, adornment, and jewelry mentioned in that passage.

They ignore the two-step plan of salvation for women found there—have a baby and be good. But they latch onto verses they can use to silence women.

Colossians 3:18-25; 4:1

In this letter to the Colossians, Paul tells wives to submit to their husbands as is fitting to the Lord. Husbands are to love their wives and not be harsh with them. Children are to obey their parents in everything. Fathers are not to destroy the psyche of their children. Slaves are to obey their masters and masters are to treat their slaves right.

There is nothing wrong with what this letter to the Colossians says about the family. For that day and culture it was fitting. However, we do not live in the first century. It is the 21st century and we live in our own culture, which we are making daily. There is no biblical reason given why we should cling to a culture of male domination, uneducated women, helpless wives and slavery.

Misuse of Titus 2:4

Another verse complementarians use to place limits on women is Titus 2:4, which says, "Then they can train the younger women to love their husbands and children. To be self-controlled and pure, to be busy at home, to be kind, and to be subject to their husbands, so that no one will malign the word of God."

That verse in Titus is the one complementarians use to justify their teaching that woman can only teach other women, and that women should not work outside the home. However, when looking at the websites of these churches, one sees that most of the support staff are women, the treasurer is a woman, and all of the day school personnel are women, making it is obvious that these women are working outside the home. Additionally, this verse tells women to be subject to their husbands.

This verse is a summation of how Christians were supposed to live among themselves, using their current situation—their NOW—to explain how to behave and live as Christians in that culture, *so that the word of God was not maligned*. Again, the purpose for Paul's writing was the gospel and removal of anything that would hinder its acceptance at that time. It was not a directive for women for all time.

That one little verse, Titus 2:4, keeps women from teaching men and acts to subdue one half of the Christian population. The verse itself does not limit women. It is the use of the verse that limits women.

When did God make man divine?

When will Christians open their eyes to see that God made women complete? How long before women understand they do not need a male to be their leader-head because God made both men and women to lead?

It bears repeating: The apostle used the marriage customs of his day to explain how Christ is the head of the church—of both men and women. This passage is not about giving men divine-like authority that frequently requires wives to close their ears to God's promptings and obey their husbands instead.

To believe otherwise makes this question necessary: When did God make man divine?

Male headship is dethroned by the scripture which says 'You shall have no other gods before Me' (Exodus 20:3).

CHAPTER 9

Qualifications of overseers and deacons

One of the most misunderstood passages of scripture in the Bible, and the one which directly affects the majority of women in both denominational and nondenominational churches, is found in 1 Timothy 3:12, "A deacon must be the husband of but one wife and must manage his children and his household well" (NIV 1984). However, the New International Version (NIV 2011) translates that verse as "A deacon must be *faithful to their spouse* and manage their children and their own households well."

Those churches that choose to deny women the office of pastor or of deacon and elder, cling to the 1984 New International Version translation of the Bible and continue to use the phrase "one woman man" in their church By-laws. For that reason, it is important to continue to approach the explanation from that view.

Bible translators interpret this passage based upon the teaching of their particular denominations or their own personal long-held beliefs. For instance, the Ryrie Study Bible of the New King James Version says this about 1 Timothy 3:12:

"Deacons. The word means 'minister,' or 'servant.' Deacons were originally the helpers of the elders. Thus their qualifications were

practically the same as those for the elders. The office had its begin-
nings in Jerusalem (Acts 6:1-6). However, the word deacon is used in
an unofficial sense throughout the New Testament of anyone who
serves (Ephesians 6:21) as well as in an official sense, designating
those who occupy the office of deacon (Philippians 1:1)."

Because the translators of the Ryrie Study Bible do not accept
women as deacons, they discredit Romans 16:1 which says, "I com-
mend to you Phoebe our sister, who is a servant of the church in
Cenchrea." Ryrie shows how she is discredited even though, according to their own translation of the word "servant," she would certainly
have the title of deacon. Ryrie says in the explanation notes, "Phoebe...a servant of the church. The word here translated 'servant' is often
translated 'deacon,' which leads some to believe that Phoebe was a
deaconess. However, the word is more likely used here in an unofficial sense of helper."

It is in this way they have chosen to diminish Phoebe's position in
the early church based upon their teaching and belief that a woman
cannot be a deacon, even though she meets their own definition of a
deacon when they say she is a "helper."

Philip B. Payne in "Examining the Twelve Biblical Pillars of Male
Hierarchy," based on his book *Man and Woman, One in Christ*, says
this about the qualifications of deacons in 1 Timothy 3, "The New
Testament names only one local church leader by office and that is
Phoebe, deacon of the church in Cenchrea" (Romans 16:1; pages 61-
63 of his book).

Since Paul himself called Phoebe a deacon, it is hard to explain the
passage as specifically limiting the office of deacon to males. In fact,
Payne says in his explanation that there are no masculine pronouns or
any other limitation to men in either list of overseers or elders. He
writes that the phrase "one woman man" excludes polygamists but
does not exclude women or unmarried men like Paul or even Jesus.

Paul was admonishing against polygamy

It is clear that Paul was telling the church to choose men who were married to only one wife at a time, likely because it would burden a family who already had many wives and children. Women have never been allowed more than one husband at a time in any society. In this passage, Paul is speaking about men having plural wives—not about being divorced—as the church has taught for centuries. The church has not chosen to recognize that down through the centuries, many men belonging to certain cultures or religious groups have had plural wives. Muslim countries allow four wives, and missionaries encounter men having multiple wives in some African countries.

Even today in the United States, there are men who want to have more than one wife. One example of this is found in the Fundamental Latter Day Saints (FLDS) where most men have multiple wives as a part of practicing their religion.

Churches in the United States, which should know better, act as if they have never heard of such a thing and cannot believe that Paul was addressing the practice of having multiple wives in one family. Fundamentalist seminaries fail to teach the truth, because the truth is inconvenient to the complementarian belief system.

Bowing to modern times regarding divorce

Refusing to relinquish the restriction of deacons and elders to males only, churches have ignored the obvious and come up with their own definition of "husband of one wife." For years they have taught that divorced men could not be deacons because they had been a husband to more than one wife. Men who were married to women who had previously been divorced were excluded also. After divorce became common, they began to include divorced men as deacons.

One church in northeast Texas posted the following on their website regarding the qualifications for deacons: "A deacon must be a one woman man. Our church recognizes divorce as an unfortunate result of sin in the world but also understands the ability of God's grace to transform and renew those who have experienced it. The phrase, 'a one woman man,' means he is not involved in sexual impurity and, if married, is committed to his present wife."

This particular church permits divorced men to be ordained as deacons but would never consider the possibility that a woman could become a deacon. To associate the scripture in 1 Timothy 3 with divorce is wrong and inexcusable. Allowing divorced men to become deacons is a compromise to today's culture and would never have been permitted by most churches in the recent past. This is not to say that divorced men or women should not be deacons, but to point out that an exception to their rule has already been made.

Both the association of this verse with divorce and the accommodation to divorced men can be found in the by-laws of many churches, but they will make no such accommodation for women as deacons. They rely upon the fact that most people do not understand that this prohibition is not about gender.

It is all about doing what is right

To determine how your church teaches, look to see if women are serving the Lord's Supper, taking up the offering collection, praying or reading scripture in the worship service, as these generally are responsibilities given to deacons. A visit to the church's website is often revealing, because many fundamental churches want people to know this is what they believe.

Church members should read the Constitution and By-laws of their churches to see what limitations the church has placed on women. *These legal documents can be changed by vote of church members.*

Paul said in 1 Timothy 3:8-10 that deacons must be moral. They must be Christians of good character. Their children must also demonstrate integrity. This whole passage in 1 Timothy 3:1-12 is about doing what is *right*. Churches have taken those words and made them all about gender.

> *Male headship is dethroned by a correct understanding of 1 Timothy 3:1-12.*

CHAPTER 10

Churches' actions dethrone male headship

Churches have skirted all around the issue of what women can do in churches, all the while withholding pulpit preaching, and, depending upon the church denomination, volunteer positions of being an elder or a deacon. These are supposed to be positions of servanthood, but down through history, the position of pastor was far more exalted than being a servant.

It is their identification of pastor that will not be given up, or shared with women. If the position as pastor is to be shared, then it will follow that elders and deacons will also surrender leadership to that of sharing with women.

Must a woman be silent?

In 1 Timothy 2:11-12, Paul wrote "A woman should learn in quietness and full submission. I do not permit a woman to teach or to have authority over a man; she must be silent."

This scripture is used as a sledgehammer over women's heads.

Considering that 10 of the 29 people Paul commended in Romans 16 are women, and were commended for teaching men, how can anyone justify interpreters who claim Paul is commanding women to be silent, have no authority, and not teach men?

The apostle Paul is not available to ask that question of him, but pastors should be asked to explain how women can be commended for leadership over men in the first century but denied leadership over men in the 21st century.

Look what some churches have decided women can do, which is contrary to a literal reading of the scriptures.

Paul says women cannot teach men, yet in some fundamental churches women teach:

- teenage boys who have begun shaving and thus considered to be men (however, in some churches women cannot teach little boys who have been baptized)
- through the written word in books, blogs, and videoed Bible studies
- through singing church solos or singing in the church choir
- Sunday school classes with both men and women discussing scripture
- men on mission fields

Paul wrote that women cannot have authority over men. Some complementarians teach that this extends to secular jobs and that women are forbidden to have supervisory positions over men. Yet in churches:

- women serve on pastor search committees
- women vote on whom to call as pastor
- women vote on church matters such as church constitutions, and by-laws
- women chair committees as designated by the church
- women are treasurers whose jobs require accountability from male staff
- women are hired to direct children, youth, adults, music, and education, which certainly include males

Paul wrote that women must be silent in the churches, yet:

- women profess their faith verbally before entire congregations
- brides stand with their husbands and vow before the church *(a strict following of the 'must be silent' rule would render Christian marriages like the Jewish ceremonies which must take place outside of the synagogue and under a tent, because the woman cannot speak in the synagogue. The groom can come down temporarily to her level and meet her in a tent, but she cannot ascend to his level.)*
- women make a joyful noise before the Lord in song
- women play the piano, which is a musical telling of the gospel
- women stand behind the pulpit and announce upcoming events
- women testify of God's working in camps and on mission trips
- women act in ministry-related skits
- women speak in spiritual tongues and shout in some churches
- women act in Christmas plays that have the sole purpose of telling the world that the Messiah has come

What about this so-called difficult scripture?

First, we must ask the question "How can the apostle Paul change, negate, or minimize what Jesus did regarding women?" The answer is that Paul cannot. Since the apostle Paul cannot supersede Jesus, we must look at the situations previously mentioned in Chapter 5 regarding Mary of Bethany, the Gentile woman, the woman at the well, and Mary at the tomb. In these accounts, Jesus gave women the most extraordinary news of who he is. How can women not tell? Who are we to deny the women Jesus calls to preach and teach?

The real difficulty in this scripture is this: that many Christians find it easier to believe that God made women inferior, than it is to believe that those scriptures have been misinterpreted. The fact that women choose not to cause disruption in the church or have been bullied into not fighting for full equality to serve God, does not make this attitude of male superiority right.

It is still sin, whether or not women demand recognition of their equality. But, as has been shown, churches cannot function without women and have made many exceptions to their own rule that "a woman must be silent."

Male headship is dethroned by the actions of the churches themselves.

CHAPTER **11**

In search of
biblical womanhood

It is impossible to discover what 'womanhood' means in the Bible. The Bible does not speak of any glory associated with being a woman, certainly nothing like the glorification of biblical womanhood that we hear in churches today. The apostle Paul makes reference to women being the glory of man in 1 Corinthians 11:7, but here he is referring to the creation story of woman being created from man. To follow through with that line of thought, the one created does not have the glory, but it is the Creator who has the glory.

So, if women are the glory of man (biblical womanhood), it is Man being glorified, not women.

Manhood and womanhood

Manhood and womanhood are not concepts found in the Bible since the words simply mean "adult male" and "adult female," and can have whatever attributes ascribed to them as is desired. Jesus said specifically that Christians should not desire to rule over others and we know from reading the Bible that Jesus never indicated that gender has anything to do with spiritual knowledge, longings, or closeness to God.

So what was it about 'biblical womanhood' that made the Council on Biblical Manhood and Womanhood decide they needed to create a whole industry of seminars, conferences, books, blogs, and preaching helps, to make women conform?

Biblical womanhood tied to 1950s era television

To find the answer, look to the timeframe that these words made their appearance by the Council on Biblical Manhood and Womanhood. It was the end of the era of television shows such as *Leave it to Beaver*, *The Donna Reed Show*, *Father Knows Best*, *Lassie*, *Leave it to Daddy*, and *The Dick Van Dyke Show*, all of which showed the ideal family of father, mother and children.

In these television shows, mothers were homemakers dressed in heels and pearls, while father went to work. This became the picture of womanhood. "Biblical womanhood" then took its *special cue* (to borrow a phrase from John Piper) from television shows, and bore little resemblance to real life.

Biblical manhood and womanhood became the terms used to hold on to an era that legally ended with the Civil Rights Act of 1964, when women were given equal rights under the law. "Biblical womanhood" embraces stay-at-home mothers as housekeepers and submissive wives. "Biblical manhood" means that men are to earn the money for food, clothing and shelter, and be the spiritual and secular leader over their wives. As previously stated, this has no biblical foundation.

There is no perfect time in human history that Christians should cling to. Every era has its mistakes and misguided theology. To bind women and men to a glorified American era, cannot speak to the world today. It is Christ that the world needs, not some prettied up picture of the past.

What does the Bible say about womanhood?

All this focused attention on the beautiful picture of biblical womanhood calls for a search through the Bible to see what the Bible says about it. Since it has its roots in the Old Testament, the search begins there.

- Is it women bearing children in pain and oftentimes giving up their own lives so that their children can be born?
- Is it the fact that the rabbi, along with every man and every woman in the community, knew when it was a woman's time of the month?
- Is biblical womanhood having a female baby and being ceremonially unclean for 14 days, with a purification time of 66 days, as opposed to having a boy and being ceremonially unclean for only 7 days with a purification time of just 33 days?
- Is it the picture of a married woman being summoned by the King to his bed, and then hearing of the death of her husband by the command of the King, her superior and by obedience, her lover?
- Is it the picture of a girl being raped by her brother and in agony enduring the shame, guilt, and distress?
- Is it the picture of Naomi who lost her sons and connived to get her daughter-in-law wed to a rich relative so they would not starve?
- Is it Jezebel who painted her face, and in doing so kept women from respectably using cosmetics for thousands of years?
- Is God's beautiful womanhood pictured in Rahab, the woman whose prostitution is forever connected to her name?
- Is it Hannah who prayed for a son and then made a vow to give up that child to the Lord as soon as he was weaned?
- Is the beautiful picture of womanhood portrayed in the story of Leah, whose father forced her to marry Jacob, who was tricked into marrying her, when Jacob really wanted Rachel, the prettier daughter?
- Is it the numerous wives and concubines with whom women shared their husbands?

What is the beautiful picture of womanhood in the New Testament?

- Is the beautiful biblical picture of womanhood found in Ephesians, Peter, and Corinthians where Paul tells women what clothes to wear, what jewelry not to wear, and to cover their heads?
- Is this beautiful picture of womanhood found in Ephesians where Paul finds it necessary to remind husbands to love their wives and, since they would not give themselves a black eye, they must not give their wives one either?

The beautiful picture of womanhood is found in Jesus' actions!

- The Council on Biblical Manhood and Womanhood has it all wrong. Biblical womanhood is what Jesus did for women. It cannot be found in restricting women to First Century dress codes, nor is it limiting women in ministry opportunities. The beautiful picture of womanhood is revealed through Jesus and is one of freedom from man-made laws and governing.
- It is found in Jesus lifting women from that "pretty picture" of womanhood when he touched her and stopped the flow of blood from a woman who had been hemorrhaging for 12 years.
- It is found in Jesus lifting women from that "pretty picture" of womanhood when he stayed the hands of the men who sought to stone a woman caught in adultery while allowing her male partner to go free.
- It is found in Jesus telling the woman at the well that he was the Messiah and seeing her run through the streets telling others this good news.
- It is found in Jesus telling the woman as she poured the alabaster vial of pure nard over his head that her story would be told forever as a memorial to her.

- It is found in Jesus welcoming Mary, a woman forbidden by culture and law from learning the scriptures from the rabbis, to sit at the feet of the Master himself.
- It is found in Jesus when he healed the Canaanite woman's daughter in a symbolic gesture telling all that Gentiles were now worthy to eat at the Lord's table.
- It is found in Jesus telling Mary at the tomb that he was risen and to go and tell.

Male headship is dethroned by Jesus who showed us the beautiful picture of womanhood, that of freedom and grace.

PART 2

THE MYTH OF BIBLICAL MANHOOD AND WOMANHOOD

There is neither Jew nor Greek, slave nor free, male nor female, for you are all one in Christ Jesus. If you belong to Christ, then you are Abraham's seed, and heirs according to the promise.

Galatians 3:28-29

CHAPTER 12

What the Danvers Statement REALLY says

The Danvers Statement on Biblical Manhood and Womanhood was the brainchild of Wayne Grudem, professor of theology and biblical studies. It originated from a discussion and eventually a paper he wrote in which he defined the Greek work *kephale* to mean having "authority over" instead of "source" as egalitarians were claiming.

That sums up the Danvers Statement very well. In Wayne Grudem's mind and intent – based upon his own words,[1] men having authority over women is the overriding theme. Never mind the fact that Jesus did not give males this authority or acknowledge in any way that men were superior to women. They claim that God decided at Creation that He would share His headship over women with all men.

By giving males authority based on gender and nothing else, the writers and proponents of the Danvers Statement reduce women to an inferior status by assigning specific "roles" based on gender. These assigned roles deny the power of the Holy Spirit.

Man-made roles do not allow for spiritual gifts. Spiritual gifts are those of natural abilities and also those of supernatural abilities (when God calls us to do something, He will equip us for that job). The Word of God did not categorize these gifts under two column headings: male and female. The Danvers Statement has categorized men and women into roles, but the scriptures do not. The scriptures they give to back up their arguments do not prove that God has given males headship or authority over females.

The Danvers Statement can be found on the Council for Biblical Manhood and Womanhood's website, on John Piper's Desiring God website, on the website of the Southwestern Baptist Theological Seminary in Fort Worth, Texas, and elsewhere. The president of Southwestern Baptist Theological Seminary at this writing is Paige Patterson who, along with his wife Dorothy Kelley Patterson, was instrumental in both the Danvers Statement and the Baptist Faith and Message 2000. The Baptist Faith and Message 2000 is the official statement of the Southern Baptist Convention and the majority of its 46,449 churches, and it has the same language and intent as the Danvers Statement.

This means that Baptist churches have adopted the essential dogma of the Danvers Statement without realizing it. That should surprise no one given that the CBMW has its headquarters in a Southern Baptist theological seminary.

It is all about keeping women under control

It is important to understand that the Danvers Statement is all about keeping women under control and keeping women from leadership in the home or church. We know this because it is included in the book *Recovering Biblical Manhood and Womanhood: A Response to Evangelical Feminism.* This book was edited by two of the founders of the Council on Biblical Manhood and Womanhood, John Piper and Wayne Grudem. The CBMW was founded in order to support male headship and male authority, and women's submission to that authority.

From the beginning of the Danvers Statement, one can see it diverging from biblical truths, based upon CBMW's biases and interpretations. Certainly there are differences in men and women other than anatomical differences. The Bible is not concerned with masculine and feminine traits. Jesus never mentions these inborn differences.

God Himself is described with both father and mother characteristics. In the New Testament, Jesus is concerned with the heart – not masculinity, not femininity, and certainly not genitalia.

The fallacies of the Danvers Statement

Much has been written exposing the fallacies of the Danvers Statement. However, it does not take a Bible scholar to see the misogyny presented in the Danvers Statement. In reading the Concerns and Affirmations, it is clear that this is a cultural document that denies the modern age in preference to biblical times with emphasis on restrictions against women.

Scriptures have been added to the document in an attempt to justify the return of families to the First Century. A clear reading of the scriptures does not justify male domination over females as a commandment law. It cannot. Jesus made one new law and it was not about male/female leadership, but about equality in loving each other: "A new command I give you: Love one another. As I have loved you, so you must love one another" (John 13:34).

Each point in the Danvers Statement begins with their belief that women are responsible for the breakdown of family and reinforces their teaching that males were created from the beginning to dominate and lead women.

Following is what the Danvers Statement says, along with this writer's interpretation of each point written in bold. The first section begins with their Concerns and the second section is their Affirmations.

Danvers Statement
on Biblical Manhood and Womanhood

In December, 1987, the newly-formed Council on Biblical Manhood and Womanhood met in Danvers, Massachusetts, to compose the Danvers Statement on Biblical Manhood and Womanhood. Prior to the listing of the actual affirmations that comprise the Danvers Statement, we have included a section detailing contemporary developments that serve as the rationale for these affirmations. We offer this statement to the evangelical world, knowing that it will stimulate healthy discussion, hoping that it will gain widespread assent.[2]

We have been moved in our purpose by the following contemporary developments which we observe with deep concern:

> 1.) The widespread uncertainty and confusion in our culture regarding the complementary differences between masculinity and femininity.

Actually, there is no uncertainly and confusion regarding men and women. Culture has changed, and no culture has ever been the perfect one, certainly not 2000 years ago. When this Danvers Statement was written, women had recently been given the right to serve on juries, to have credit in their names, to buy and sell a house in their own names, to make legal decisions, and to work in what was previously male dominated fields.

Some churches were even ordaining women! These are rights we take for granted in 2015, but were denied women before the Civil Rights Act of 1964. During the 20 years before the Danvers Statement was written, women had had to fight their way through the courts to attain these rights that were legally theirs, and it was cases of women winning this struggle that brought on the Danvers Statement. They desired to put a stop to women advancing in the educational and religious sectors.

> 2.) The tragic effects of this confusion in unraveling the fabric of marriage woven by God out of the beautiful and diverse strands of manhood and womanhood.

They saw women attaining higher education and now, by law, they could not be denied jobs based on their gender. This caused

their fear that women would forget what they saw as a "woman's place" in the home, and under the control of their husbands. When women became supervisors over men, or held any position that gave them authority over men, the writers of the Danvers Statement decided those actions were destroying marriages.

They were worried that women who had supervised men in the workplace during the day would not be content to be submissive wives when they came home at night.

3.) The increasing promotion given to feminist egalitarianism with accompanying distortions or neglect of the glad harmony portrayed in Scripture between the loving, humble, leadership of redeemed husbands and the intelligent, willing, support of that leadership by redeemed wives.

The word feminism still carries a negative reaction in the Christian and secular world. This explosive word "feminist" was used deliberately to associate abortion with egalitarians, even though egalitarians do not approve of abortion.

They use the phrase "glad harmony" which completely ignores the fact that the Bible says nothing about "glad harmony" in marriage. The Apostle Paul stopped in the middle of his discourse in Ephesians 5 to tell husbands they should love their wives and to treat their wives like they would their own body – in other words, feed and care for her and not abuse her. Glad harmony – hardly!

This Concern #3 is the perfect description of a one-way marriage—his way. Everything she does is to support him and build him up. However, if he is the spiritual leader, it would appear that it is his job to build up and support his wife, not the other way around.

4.) The widespread ambivalence regarding the values of motherhood, vocational homemaking, and the many ministries historically performed by women.

This Concern is that women will not want to be stay-at-home mothers and church volunteers. What they are saying is that a woman's place is in the home and not in the workplace or in church leadership.

What they do not say is that women who work outside the home are also vocational homemakers, in addition to spending many hours volunteering in the church. Ignored is the fact that these working mothers are often the difference between hungry children and fed children.

5.) The growing claims of legitimacy for sexual relationships which have Biblically and historically been considered illicit or perverse and the increase in pornographic portrayal of human sexuality.

At first reading this would not appear to have women as the basis of their Concern. However, the rise in homosexuality (perverse relationship) is blamed on women by the Council on Biblical Manhood and Womanhood, as is found on their website:

Egalitarianism and Homosexuality.[3] It is increasingly and painfully clear that Biblical feminism is an unwitting partner in unraveling the fabric of complementary manhood and womanhood that provides the foundation not only for Biblical marriage and Biblical church order, but also for heterosexuality itself.

Reread that sentence above. This is what it says: *women who desire equality are destroying marriages, churches, and heterosexuality.* Why is it that women are blamed for destroying marriages and churches, without the complicity of males? How can women destroy heterosexuality? The apostle Paul was not as harsh as this! Also, in Chapter 18, "Sexualizing the Trinity," we see it is pastors themselves who are indulging in pornographic portrayals of the church.

6.) The upsurge of physical and emotional abuse in the family.

Wives are responsible for being abused, both physically and emotionally if one believes what Bruce Ware said,

"And husbands on their parts, because they're sinners, now respond to that threat to their authority either by being abusive, which is of course one of the ways men can respond when their authority is challenged—or, more commonly, to become passive, acquiescent, and simply not asserting the leadership they ought to as men in their homes and in churches."[4]

In that sentence, an excuse is given for physical (beatings) and emotional abuse against wives and mothers.

7.) The emergence of roles for men and women in church leadership that do not conform to Biblical teaching but backfire in the crippling of Biblically faithful witness.

This Concern is that some churches have begun ordaining women to roles in church leadership that men have always held – pastors, deacons, elders – and that somehow this will destroy the church.

The church is shrinking but it is not because of women being ordained. It is the status quo that is shrinking churches and a loss of spiritual vision. Ordaining women across all denominations would see a spiritual revival like has not been seen in recent memory.

8.) The increasing prevalence and acceptance of hermeneutical oddities devised to reinterpret apparently plain meanings of Biblical Texts.

What they are saying is that the plain English reading of certain scriptures give men headship and authority over women (you can be assured that they are not concerned about any other scriptures). However, the scriptures they quote that they say gives man headship, are not supported by the Jesus who is found in the Gospels. There is no scripture, or quote, or action by Jesus that would back up the belief that men have headship over women.

9.) The consequent threat to Biblical authority as the clarity of Scripture is jeopardized and the accessibility of its meaning to ordinary people is withdrawn into the restricted realm of technical ingenuity.

This Concern reinforces their belief that women are inferior to males, and claims that to say differently is a threat to Biblical authority. It is notable, again, that Jesus gave no indication of male superiority over females.

10.) And behind all this the apparent accommodation of some within the church to the spirit of the age at the expense of winsome, radical Biblical authenticity which in the power of the Holy Spirit may reform rather than reflect our ailing culture.

Again, the ailing culture, according to this Concern of the Council on Biblical Manhood and Womanhood, is caused by women who desire to be equal. It appears to be important to bring back "the good ole days" and they call upon the Holy Spirit to put women in their place (to reform).

In this list of their 10 Concerns, the blame is placed on women who desire the equality given them by God and stolen from them

by man. Women are painted as destroying churches, marriages, and the ideal culture, and therefore must be brought under control by the church and husbands. They have blamed women for every concern they list.

Affirmations

Based on our understanding of Biblical teachings, we affirm the following:

1.) Both Adam and Eve were created in God's image, equal before God as persons and distinct in their manhood and womanhood (Genesis 1:26-27; 2:18).

What they do not tell us is why they feel male bodies are superior to female bodies, because if women and men are equal as persons, that means it is the physical male body that is distinctly superior. Make no mistake about it. They find the maleness of humanity superior.

2.) Distinctions in masculine and feminine roles are ordained by God as part of the created order and should find an echo in every human heart (Genesis 2:18, 21-24; 1 Corinthians 11:7-9; 2:12-14).

Thump, thump. The only echo here is when they tell us that men were created superior and women inferior. They have repeated it too many times. There is no justification for teaching that men were designed to have authority over women. The created order has nothing to do with it and is a red herring to make it sound good.

To nail down masculine roles is difficult and to nail down feminine roles is even harder. To simplify it, masculine roles are anything men desire to do, while women's roles are what men have decided women can do.

3.) Adam's headship in marriage was established by God before the Fall and was not a result of sin (Genesis 2:16-18, 21-24, 3:1-13; 1 Corinthians 11:7-9).

What cannot be found anywhere in the Bible is the scripture that explains why women need to be ruled over, either before or after the Fall. What also cannot be found in the scripture is where Adam was capable of ruling over a serpent, much less a woman. When they were given the task of subduing the creatures, Eve was right there beside Adam. As we know, Adam failed the very first task of subduing the serpent.

4.) The Fall introduced distortions into the relationships between men and women (Genesis 3:1-7, 12, 16). In the home, the husband's loving, humble headship tends to be replaced by domination or passivity; the wife's intelligent, willing submission tends to be replaced by usurpation or servility. In the Church, sin inclines men toward a worldly love of power or an abdication of spiritual responsibility, and inclines women to resist limitation on their roles or to neglect the use of their gifts in appropriate ministries.

They indicate men are wimps and blame it on the Fall. That is school-yard bullying. And they hope no one will notice that they are the ones who give men all the power, thus feeding men's inclination to rule over women, even though it is common knowledge that power corrupts. They say that the relationship between men and women in the church is distorted because sin makes men love power or neglect their spiritual responsibility, and causes women to resist the limits man has placed upon them.

Neither before nor after the Fall, did Adam show any spiritual responsibility! He didn't have to because he was not given any spiritual responsibility over Eve. Go back and read the scriptures. Adam and Eve were to subdue the animals together. Adam was

not instructed to subdue his wife, nor was Eve instructed to follow his lead.

They could not find a scripture that backed up what they teach, but they used those scriptures anyway thinking no one would notice.

God said "Adam, where are you?" Silence from Adam as he and Eve hunker down beneath a fig tree. Finally Adam says, "I heard you but I was afraid and I was naked. The woman you put here with me, she gave me some fruit from the tree, and I ate it."

Try to find where Adam, from the time he was formed, demonstrated any spiritual responsibility. Eve did, though. She admitted to God, "The serpent deceived me and I ate." Repentance. She did not blame Adam for not showing spiritual responsibility. She did not say that his loving, humble headship did not rise to the occasion.

Because Eve was a strong woman, one who shouldered the responsibility and repented of the sin, the church has used this against her ever since. Eve took charge. That is the distortion they are talking about. Men are to model themselves after Adam who ratted out his wife, hid with her, and acted like she was something that God had foisted upon him.

They want us to believe that Eve's sin inclines women to resist being limited in their "roles." They are worried that women might want to use their spiritual gifts of leadership in preaching and pastoring. Their attitude diminishes both men and women. This teaching diminishes men by not holding them accountable for their actions (like Adam's), and diminishes women by telling them that they cannot stand up and give spiritual leadership (like Eve did).

5.) The Old Testament, as well as the New Testament, manifests the equally high value and dignity which God attached to the roles of both men and women (Genesis 1:26-27, 2:1; Galatians 3:28). Both Old and New Testaments also affirm the principle of male headship in the family and in the covenant community (Genesis 2:18; Ephesians 5:21- 33; Colossians 3:18-19; 1 Timothy 2:11-15).

Well, of course that is one big distortion of all those texts, starting with Genesis and ending with Timothy. Adam was created first, and that is the only thing he had going for him. Is that enough? He demonstrated no loving, humble leadership, no bravery, no protection or support of Eve. Nothing—only that he got here first. There is not one example of headship in any of those verses they quote.

Colossians 3:18-25; 4:1 is a reminder for families to live in peace with one another: wives, husbands, children, slaves and masters (Colossians 3:15). The oft quoted Ephesians passage finds Paul having to tell the men to love their wives. Women have been told for centuries that they are the ones who must be pure and without stain (sexual sin) or wrinkle or any other blemish (Ephesians 5:27).

These men had to be commanded to simply *love* their wives as they would their own bodies, which meant they had not been doing a good job of loving their wives.

There is nothing about roles in those scriptures. Role is a word meaning to act a part in a particular situation. Roles can and do change. God did not assign roles. Man assigns roles depending upon what outcome is desired at the time.

According to the complementarian interpretation of 1 Timothy 2:11-12, men are not required to have any leadership qualification whatsoever; what a leader must have is male genitalia. That is not very flattering, and not what Christianity should be centered around.

6.) Redemption in Christ aims at removing the distortions introduced by the curse.

That is a made-up, distorted theology. Redemption in Christ has nothing to do with male and female relationships. Redemption is about healing both men's and women's relationship to God.

> In the family, husbands should forsake harsh or selfish leadership and grow in love and care for their wives; wives should forsake resistance to their husbands' authority and grow in willing, joyful submission to their husbands' leadership (Ephesians 5:21-33; Colossians 3:18-19; Titus 2:3-5; 1 Peter 3:1-7).

A better statement by the Council would have simply read: "Husbands and wives should respect and love each other and raise their children to love the Lord, as they themselves do." However, they did not do that. That would have endorsed female equality and would have negated the entire Danvers Statement. So let's continue with what they did say.

The simple reading of these scriptures instructs wives to submit to their husbands. The Council apparently realized there was a problem with this and decided to pretty it up. Leadership is not mentioned in the scriptures they give. And, even though men are told to love their wives and not harm them, in actuality, a husband can be in love with his wife and still physically and emotionally harm her.

Another problem is that these scriptures do not instruct women in how to accept the authority of her husband, which is not surprising since these scriptures do not give a husband authority.

For centuries men have allowed no exceptions to these scriptures, and if these scriptures are followed as written, it means wives are to submit to their husbands in any and all situations, and to any and all men who are husbands, redeemed or not, and harsh or not.

Men and governments have used these scriptures against women and have allowed wives to be abused, both physically and mentally. Many husbands who do not even attend church, abuse their wives based on these scriptures. There are instances of pastors telling women that they must submit to certain levels of abuse, including physical abuse, because women are to submit to their husbands, redeemed or not.

Wives do not need to be under the authority of a husband-leader. What man wants a wife-child as a companion? The woman Adam was given in the Garden was a companion fully grown and fully responsible. It is our children who need leaders—the leadership of both mothers and fathers.

> In the church, redemption in Christ gives men and women an equal share in the blessings of salvation; nevertheless, some governing and teaching roles within the church are restricted to men (Galatians 3:28:28; 1 Corinthians 11:2-16; 2:11-15).

They do not deny that women can receive salvation; it is just that women's salvation comes with restrictions. According to Bruce Ware, a woman's salvation comes first by accepting the "role" he says God gave her, and then by accepting God.[4]

This is where they tell women that they cannot do this and cannot do that in church. Of course each church decides exactly what *this and that* means. One rule of thumb is to see what the church considers "important" work, and that is for men; the rest can be done by either women or men.

> 7.) In all of life Christ is the supreme authority and guide for men and women, so that no earthly submission—domestic, religious, or civil—ever implies a mandate to follow a human authority into sin (Daniel 3:10-18; Acts 4:19-20; 5:27-29; 1 Peter 3:1-2).

According to the CBMW, the woman is supposed to determine if her leader-husband is asking her to sin. This puts no accountability on the husband. It all becomes her problem. This woman who has to be led, now has to be able to recognize and determine if what she is being led to do is a sin.

This Affirmation is really strange in that it contradicts "male headship" because it puts a limit on what males can demand. They say that wives are exempt from engaging in sinful demands by their husbands. However, the very word and concept of male headship is that males make the rules for their wives, and they set the parameters for female obedience.

This is affirmed by Dorothy Patterson, one of the founders of CBMW and the wife of Paige Patterson who is also a founder of CBMW, when she said, "As a woman standing under the authority of Scripture, even when it comes to submitting to my husband when I know he's wrong, I just have to do it, and then he stands accountable at the judgment." From Dorothy Patterson's statement, it appears that she *must* follow her husband into sin if that is what he asks of her.

8.) In both men and women, a heartfelt sense of call to the ministry should never be used to set aside Biblical criteria for particular ministries (1 Timothy 2:11-15, 3:1-13; Titus 1:5-9). Rather, Biblical teaching should remain the authority for testing our subjective discernment of God's will.

If a woman is called to preach or serve in some other leadership capacity, she must deny that call because, according to the Council, God cannot call a woman to preach. Men are never called upon to set aside their heartfelt sense of a call because of their gender.

9.) With half the world's population outside the reach of indigenous evangelism; with countless other lost people in those societies have heard the gospel; with the stresses and miseries of sickness, malnutrition, homelessness, illiteracy, ignorance, aging, addiction, crime, incarceration, neuroses, and loneliness, no man or woman who feels a passion from God to make His grace known in word and deed need ever live without a fulfilling ministry for the glory of Christ and the good of this fallen world (1 Corinthians 12:7-21).

Look at the hypocrisy and condescending attitude here. They are willing to allow women to go out into the gutters of the streets where the homeless, drug addicts, and criminals are, but will not allow them to serve behind the safety of a pulpit.

They will send women to foreign mission fields where the people are often darker and do not speak the same language. A woman said after the SBC missionary commissioning service of her granddaughter, "How can they send girls out to these dangerous places?" Yet they do. But they will keep the white, English-speaking churches for males.

Jesus saw the whole world as a field to harvest, and called for laborers. Then he said to his disciples, "The harvest is plentiful but the workers are few. Ask the Lord of the harvest, therefore, to send out workers into his harvest field" (Matthew 9:37).

The Council finds it all right to send women missionaries to dangerous places in the world, even though they teach that women are unable to protect their families or themselves. It is a testimony to women and their love for God that they are willing to serve wherever they are called. It is a testimony *against* restrictive churches that decide that women can *only* be called to serve in a church far away from their homes and families.

10.) We are convinced that a denial or neglect of these principles will lead to increasingly destructive consequences in our families, our churches, and the culture at large.

According to the Danvers Statement written by the Council on Biblical Manhood and Womanhood, whatever happens to families, churches, and culture depends upon the willful decision that women make of whether or not they will submit to male domination. In their prediction, any decision other than to submit to male domination will lead to the destruction: 1) of the authority of scripture; 2) of the home; 3) of the church; 4) of worship; 5) of Bible translations; 6) and of the gospel. This is found on their website under Mission and Vision.

The Council on Biblical Manhood and Womanhood has it wrong

The Council on Biblical Manhood and Womanhood's teaching is completely outside anything that Jesus said or did. Jesus held individuals responsible for their own actions. In no way did Jesus hold women accountable for the deeds of men. Likewise, Jesus did not hold men accountable for the deeds of women.

It was not wives whom Jesus held responsible for the destruction of worship and family. It was the religious leaders – the ones who stood before the people – whom he held responsible.

While they quote many scriptures, none back up male headship or a husband's authority over his wife. Jesus is not quoted in any of the scriptures given by the Council on Biblical Manhood and Womanhood.

PART 3

DEMAND FOR AN APOLOGY FROM THE COUNCIL ON BIBLICAL MANHOOD AND WOMANHOOD

Woe to you, teachers of the law and Pharisees, you hypocrites! You are like whitewashed tombs, which look beautiful on the outside but on the inside are full of dead men's bones and everything unclean. In the same way, on the outside you appear to people as righteous but on the inside you are full of hypocrisy and wickedness.

Matthew 23:27-28

CHAPTER 13

Apology Demand

Apology Demanded from the
Council on Biblical Manhood and Biblical Womanhood

The following "Apology Demand"[1] letter was drafted by Co-founders of the Freedom for Christian Women Coalition, Shirley Taylor, founder of bWe Baptist Women for Equality and Jocelyn Andersen, author of *Woman this is WAR! Gender, Slavery and the Evangelical Caste System.* It was presented live and via video at the Seneca Falls 2 Christian Women's Rights Convention held in Orlando, Florida on July 24, 2010.

Taylor and Andersen, along with seven others, signed the Demand, and On July 26, 2010, sent it by FedEx to Dr. Randy Stinson, President Council on Biblical Manhood and Womanhood, and to Dr. J Ligon Duncan III, Chairman of the Board of the CBMW.

Directed to the
Council for Biblical Manhood and Womanhood from
the Freedom for Christian Women Coalition

At a time in our church history that the main focus should be on winning lost souls and spreading the gospel to a hurting world, we fear for the future because the Council on Biblical Manhood and

Womanhood has placed a greater priority on women's submissive roles rather than on the gospel of Jesus Christ.

It is with that thought in mind that we make the following statements:

1.) We are concerned that men are being taught that they are god-like in their relationship to women within the church and home. As the mothers, wives, and daughters of these men, it is our concern that this doctrine is setting them up for failure as Christian fathers, husbands, and sons.

2.) We are concerned about the sin that evangelical church leaders commit when they deny the love of Christ fully to women simply because they were born female.

3.) We are concerned about the damage this causes to families when husbands and fathers are told that they have headship over their wives and daughters.

4.) We are concerned about wife abuse, girlfriend abuse, and abuse to female children that takes place in many homes where evangelical men are taught that they have earthly and spiritual authority over women.

5.) We are concerned that the children who attend churches that have adopted the Danvers Statement on Biblical Manhood and Womanhood will grow up not knowing the full redemptive power of the blood of Jesus for both men and women.

6.) We are concerned for the mental and emotional development of the girls and boys who attend churches that teach that males have superiority over females.

7.) We are concerned that men who are taught that they have Male Headship over a home and church feel they are not accountable for abusive attitudes and actions towards women.

8.) We are concerned about the mistranslation of scriptures by complementarian translation committees and by the false teachings propagated by the Council on Biblical Manhood and Womanhood.

9.) We are concerned that pastors who teach and preach male domination/female subordination cannot relate in a loving, Christ-like manner to female members of their congregations because they have already judged them and found them lacking.

10). We are concerned that the issue of wifely submission, promoted by the Council on Biblical Manhood and Womanhood, is more about power and control than about love or obeying the Word of God.

It is Because of These Concerns That:

1.) We demand that the Council on Biblical Manhood and Womanhood acknowledge the harm that has been done to the church by the Danvers Statement on Biblical Manhood and Womanhood, and confess it as sin, and renounce it.

2.) We demand that denominational leaders and all churches and seminaries which have adopted the Danvers Statement on Biblical Manhood and Biblical Womanhood do the same.

3.) We demand a public apology from the Council on Biblical Manhood and Womanhood and from all heads of seminaries and Bible colleges that have adopted the Danvers Statement on Biblical Manhood and Womanhood for the inestimable damage this statement has done to all Christians whose lives have been influenced by it.

4.) We demand that the Council on Biblical Manhood and Womanhood begin to promote the Biblical design of functional equality for all Christians alike, both men and women.

5.) We demand that the Council on Biblical Manhood and Womanhood begin to speak out against pastors who continue to demean women and oppress Christians by the use of the Danvers Statement on Biblical Manhood and Womanhood.

6.) We demand that the Council on Biblical Manhood and Womanhood chastise pastors who claim that abuse of women is acceptable and is justified because the wife is not submitting to the husband.

7.) We demand that the Council on Biblical Manhood and Womanhood make known to every boy and every girl who attends an evangelical church, that God is their head—equally, and that God has not granted males authority over females.

8.) We demand that the Council on Biblical Manhood and Womanhood teach men that they share equally in the burden of society's ills, and that all that is wrong with society today cannot be blamed on women.

9.) We demand that the Council on Biblical Manhood and Womanhood do everything in their power to teach seminarians to show the love of Christ to both men and women.

10.) We demand that the Council on Biblical Manhood and Womanhood teach pastors to be loving towards those Christian men and women who disagree with the Danvers Statement on Biblical Manhood and Womanhood.

11.) And, finally, for the sake of all Christians, both men and women, we demand that the Council on Biblical Manhood and Womanhood make a public apology for the misuse of Holy Scripture as it relates to women and cease to publish or promote the Danvers Statement on Biblical Manhood and Womanhood.

PART 4

MALE HEADSHIP MUST BE DETHRONED

It was Mary Magdalene, Joanna, Mary the mother of James, and the others with them who told this to the apostles. But they did not believe the women, because their words seemed to them like nonsense.

Luke 24:10-12

CHAPTER 14

What male headship means

Male headship means that *all* males have authority over *all* females *all of* the time. It is commonly referred to as leadership, because even complementarians realize how ridiculous male headship sounds.

Among Christians, there are two generally accepted views on how women are to be treated in the church and also in the home. Each view has variations as some adherents are more restrictive than others. The majority of Christians have never considered themselves to be either complementarian or egalitarian. However, whichever teaching a church or denomination subscribes to, one of those terms would apply.

Women are either equal or they are not

Even in society at large, women fit into one of these categories. There cannot be a half-way measure. Either women are equal or they are not. Most of the world has decided that women are not equal. We cannot change the whole world, but Christians have a responsibility to be like Jesus, and that means treating women with love as equals instead of with contempt and superiority.

As previously explained, complementarian is a word coined by the writers of the Danvers Statement to describe their teaching which they believe sets the guidelines for how men and women best complete or complement each other. It means that men and women have certain roles which they claim define manhood and womanhood. A man's role is to have authority over his wife and to have authority in the home and church. A woman's role is to be submissive to, and support-ive of, her husband. She must follow her husband's leadership in eve-rything. Because of this teaching about the family, women cannot have authority over men in church. Some complementarians insist that women are to refrain from assuming authority over men even in the workplace.

The wife's "role" of submission is praised and glorified. She is told that she is equal-but. Equal, but according to something they call God's grand design, she is to have a lesser position in the church, in her own home, and even before her children. Men and women who are unmarried must also adhere to the roles prescribed for their gender, which consist of leadership and authority for males, and submissive-ness for females. This teaching keeps women in a permanent subordi-nate role.

How to determine if a church is complementarian

When a church does not have women deacons or elders it is more than likely a complementarian church, even if the church never uses the word. If a pastor evades the question when asked what position the church takes, it is very likely the church is complementarian. Male headship and denial of certain positions for women in the church go hand-in-hand.

Many evangelical denominations are complementarian in teaching. Most fundamentalist churches are complementarian churches because their women-limiting teaching is based upon what they claim is a lit-eral interpretation of the Bible.

The majority of Southern Baptist Convention churches are complementarian. The Baptist Faith and Message 2000 epitomizes complementarian teaching in Southern Baptist churches. This state-ment of faith was approved by the Southern Baptist Convention (SBC) in the year 2000, thus the name. In most SBC churches, it replaced the Baptist Faith and Message 1963 which had *no restrictions against women being pastors nor did it say that wives must submit to their husbands' leadership.* Although the Baptist Faith and Message 2000 is not accepted by all Southern Baptist churches, most SBC churches practice the restrictions against women found there and will not ordain women as deacons or pastors.

The numbers are staggering

The sheer numbers of those committed to complementarian theology are staggering. The SBC claims over 15,500,000 in their 46,449 churches in America alone. In addition, the complementarian influence extends internationally through SBC missionaries who are forced to sign the Baptist Faith and Message 2000.

The Danvers Statement's influence extends into other denominations and beyond. Although Southern Baptists are the largest group accepting the Danvers Statement, they are by no means the only group that teaches male headship. Far too many other evangelical denominations followed the lead of the SBC and adopted the teachings of complementarianism.

Campus Crusade for Christ, now with over 25,000 full-time missionaries in 181 countries, has adopted the Baptist Faith and Message 2000 and the Danvers Statement. Other prominent complementarian organizations are LifeWay Resources, Acts 29, Focus on the Family, Provident Films, Liberty University, Hope Academy, Christian publishing houses, booksellers, and locally owned Christian bookstores.

Concern for families is admirable, but they have chosen the wrong solution. It takes both a strong mother *and* father to raise children. Strong families are not made by weakening the mother of the family by requiring her to submit to the children's father.

Nondenominational churches, along with Pentecostal and some relatively few Baptist churches often have husband-wife co-pastoring teams, but they cannot all be construed as being egalitarian churches, because it is usually the husband who is senior pastor. Pentecostal and Assemblies of God churches, both leaders in allowing women senior pastors at one time, have few today because they, too, teach that husbands have headship over wives. As one Pentecostal woman said "my husband is the ruler of our home." Their children are grown and have left home, but the ruler still has her in the home to rule over.

Southern Baptist Convention is complementarian

In May 2003, more than 77 SBC missionaries left the SBC International Mission field of their own free will, or were fired, because they could not in good conscience sign the Baptist Faith and Message 2000. Missionaries, both men and women, had to either sign the document or give up their call to missions and go home. Many went home because they could not sign it, and if they desired to continue in Baptist ministries, they had to seek employment where signing the document was not a requirement. This severely limited the employment opportunities for those former Southern Baptist missionaries.

Surprisingly, there are many Southern Baptist women missionaries on the mission field today, even though they, too, have signed the document that says "the office of pastor is limited to men as qualified by Scripture."

All six Southern Baptist Convention seminaries and their 49 satellite campuses require their faculties to sign the Baptist Faith and Message 2000. So, too, the Southern Baptists of Texas Convention (SBTC) requires that their affiliated churches sign the Baptist Faith and Message 2000. The SBTC broke away from Baptist General Convention of Texas in 1998 to form a competing and more fundamental state convention. The largest churches in Texas either helped form or have affiliated with this fundamental group.

In August 2015, the Hispanic Baptist Pastors Alliance aligned behind the BF&M2000 with their 42 Southern Baptist churches in 15 states, Canada and Puerto Rico.

Paige Patterson, one of the founders of the CBMW who also helped compose the Baptist Faith and Message 2000, as of this writing, is president of Southwestern Baptist Theological Seminary. On October 27, 2011, he officiated at the signing of the BF&M 2000 at Truett-McConnell College in Tennessee.[1] The importance of this document to Southern Baptists can be found in his remarks as he presided over the signing of the BF&M 2000, "Better be dead, better never to be remembered on this earth, than to fail to be true to that document which you have signed."

That is a heavy load to place on anyone. Additionally, it gives the importance of the Baptist Faith and Message 2000 a far greater eternal significance than any document – with the exception of the Bible – should have.

Seminaries embrace the Danvers Statement

The Danvers Statement is the Council on Biblical Manhood and Womanhood's charter statement and now three of the six Southern Baptist seminaries have adopted it. The most recent adoption was in April 2015 by Midwestern Baptist Theological Seminary in St. Louis, Missouri. In October 2009, the Danvers Statement was adopted by the Southwestern Baptist Theological Seminary (SWBTS) in Fort Worth, Texas. They are the largest of the six SBC seminaries, so their adoption of the Danvers Statement makes it clear that most Baptists believe that men are elected by God to have "headship" over women. At least one of the smaller SBC seminaries, Southeastern Baptist Theological Seminary, was already using it as their affirmed statement. This document has but one purpose, and that is to convince Christian women to surrender to male control in the church and in the home.

Subscribing to the notion that all men are born leaders, and all that is needed for them to step up to that role is a little coaching, classes are taught at some SBC seminaries in how to get men to lead and women to follow. Pastors who are taught this as seminarians will naturally view women as being inferior to males when it comes to counseling women in church ministries and with family problems. Women counseled by these types of pastors are often led to believe it is their fault when their marriages begin to fail.

Danvers Statement and physical abuse

In June 2008, at a Bible church in Denton, Texas, Bruce Ware, introduced previously as a founding member of the Council on Biblical

Manhood and Womanhood, said, "And husbands on their parts, because they're sinners, now respond to that threat to their authority either by being abusive, which is of course one of the ways men can respond when their authority is challenged—or, more commonly, to become passive, acquiescent, and simply not asserting the leadership they ought to as men in their homes and in churches."[2]

Ware is the professor of Christian Theology at Southern Baptist Theological Seminary in Louisville, Kentucky. In his statement he gave husbands an excuse for abusing their wives—that of being a sinner, as if sinners are not to be held accountable.

Ware says in effect that men can do one of two things when wives do not submit: they can become abusive, or they can become meek and passive. While this is shocking to us, it is more so when we realize that this is exactly the language of the Danvers Statement in their Affirmations. Affirmation #4 says "In the home, the husband's loving, humble headship tends to be replaced by domination or passivity."

When men in that congregation heard Ware say that men can choose to abuse their wives, every man in that congregation should have stood up and said "Not my daughter, he won't!"

They did not. But you can. Stand up and say, "No man has the excuse to abuse my daughter for any reason, even if he thinks she is not submitting enough."

This "headship" teaching causes suffering, because there is no way men, or women for that matter, can have the kind of god-like power that the Danvers Statement and the Baptist Faith and Message 2000 bestows without it having dangerous consequences as seen by Ware's statement.

The teaching that goes directly into homes

This is a teaching that directly impacts homes, subjecting whole families to whatever kinds of leadership husbands decide they are divinely entitled to. The BF&M 2000 Section on the Family says "A wife is to submit herself graciously to the servant leadership of her husband."

When men are taught they have authority over women, this complementarian teaching that was born in churches and nurtured in Christian families, bleeds out into society. Both men and women who never go to church are influenced by it. Often it results in abuse of wives and girlfriends in both church and society.

Wives lose their status in marriage and come under the domination of the husband to whatever degree of submission he decides he wants. Girls are raped, sex trafficked, beaten, and murdered because females have been devalued. This devaluation produces long-term detrimental effects, and women and families suffer because of it.

Because complementarians push second-class citizenship for women in churches, when they advocate for abused women in shelters they come across as hypocrites. Church ministries spend time and money bandaging the wounds of those afflicted by male dominance, but they will not address the teaching that causes it. As Jesus said, "they will not lift a finger" to change it. In fact, they continue to perpetuate it.

Church has no authority over wife or child abusers

The Council on Biblical Manhood and Womanhood claims that they do not advocate abuse against wives, but when it does happen, they say that the church is better able to handle such domestic abuse than the secular world.

The fact is that the church has no such ability to handle abuse, and since the majority of pastors teach male headship, many will take the husband's side. They have no binding or legal authority over any member of the church and abusers cannot be held accountable in a church setting.

The only action a church can take is to tell the abuser he cannot come back to church. They cannot make him attend any program for counseling, nor can they provide legal counsel to the wife. The result is that the abuser goes free and the woman is still at the mercy of her attacker.

If the Christian church did have authority over wife abusers and family matters, this would be akin to Sharia Law, which is the legal framework of public and private life that is regulated for those living in a legal system based on Islam.

Significantly, the church also has no authority over a child abuser. The church is unable to dictate terms of compliance with the law or counseling. They have no legal authority other than to provide an "eyes on" when a predator becomes a member of their church. A family member who is being abused by another family member also cannot be protected by the church. These are cases for civil authorities and the church must not interfere with their process in handling abuse by or against church members.

How complementarianism affects individuals

It is likely that your pastor has his degree from a Southern Baptist Convention seminary. Or perhaps the degree was from a seminary with teachers who studied at an SBC seminary. It is also likely that your youth minister has his or her degree from one of these seminaries that ardently teach male headship. They will teach this to the youth groups in churches they serve. This teaching will affect attitudes and beliefs of the young men your daughters will marry.

Young girls and women will be told they are mistaken if they think God is calling them into ministry. Teenage girls will learn that their membership in churches – the body of Christ - comes with re-strictions.

However, the implications of complementarianism are far greater than what goes on in churches and on the mission field. Churches are made up of people and those church members who firmly believe in adherence to those doctrines carry that belief of male headship into the workplace, and out into society. They fail to promote women to higher paid positions because they believe women should be at home, or, particularly in private and smaller businesses, they are likely to harass and abuse women in the workplace.

Can they all be wrong?

Can they all be wrong? The answer is YES. When one group presents a rotten apple as being desirable, and others bite into it and call it sweet, does that make the rotten apple sweet? This writer is not the first, nor will she be the last, to point out that the complementarian view of men and women is not a biblical view. There are many voices crying out in protest that scriptures have been misused and mistranslated in favor of man's superiority over woman.

Civilizations change and move forward. For well over a thousand years Christ was lost among civilizations, including our own, that sought to enslave others because some believed that they were born to a higher status. The end to slavery did not come about easily because many people used the scriptures to justify owning other human beings.

The concept of male divinity is not new. Greek mythology often has superior males called gods who come to earth and mates with earthly females. Similarly, for centuries it was believed that emperors were divine. That is what is happening today with male headship, but to a greater degree than ever before. Complementarians have decided that it is not just *some* men who are born to rule over women, but that *all* men are born to rule over all women.

CHAPTER 15

Male headship distorts marriage

There has been a progression of teaching from the Council on Biblical Manhood and Womanhood which places unwarranted emphasis on what they claim is the role of men and women in marriages. They have distorted the scriptures to give males a place in the Godhead but deny this is so.

Complementarian teaching has changed a basic tenet of Christianity, that of a personal relationship with Christ. Husbands have become a bridge to heaven, a way of salvation for their wives. Whether or not, in the minds of some, marriage becomes the instrument of salvation depends upon what individual Christians ultimately do with complementarian teaching.

Husbands cannot be the 'bridge builders'

Christ has been pushed aside in favor of men (husbands) who are told they are vicars of Christ. Protestants have accused the Roman Catholic Church of taking two scripture verses, Matthew 16:18-19, and creating a religious hierarchy with man-made rules which do nothing to reflect Christ. Complementarians are now doing the same thing with marriage roles.

The Roman Catholic Church claims the Pope is Christ's representative on earth, with all the power and authority Christ had (with earthly physical limitations), and uses that as leverage over all Roman Catholics. Because of this teaching about Matthew 16:18-19, Catholics believe their Church has dominion over their souls.

In addition, Catholics give money to get their loved ones out of purgatory and for prayers to be answered because they are convinced the prayers of priests have power to change things in heaven. They are also convinced they can never attain salvation if they do not meet conditions decided upon by their Pontiff, the Pope, who is said to speak for Christ Himself.

The word Pontiff comes from a Latin word meaning "bridge builder." The Pope is their bridge (pontiff) to heaven.

Complementarianism teaches that Christ submits to God in heaven, while the husband (Christ's representative) submits to Christ, and the wife (representing the church) submits to her husband. The husband becomes her 'pontiff.' In other words, they designate the husband as having become part of the divinity, with the right of rulership, so he can command obedience from his wife.

Husbands as mediators between wives and God

The complementarian wife is powerless to choose her own direction, or to hear from God for herself, unless it agrees with what her so-called spiritual leader, her husband, says. Her divine husband becomes her mediator, taking the place of Jesus as leader in her life.

They can teach this because they have decided that the husband plays the part of Jesus in a marriage, and they see no contradiction to 1 Timothy 2:5 which says, "For there is one God and one mediator between God and men (humankind), the man Christ Jesus." She must submit to her husband and obey him in everything. In this manner, it is not the church, which is made up of both men and women, that is the body of Christ, it is wives who become the body of Christ, and husbands who replace Christ's leadership.

Husbands cannot be mediators

If a husband *could* be given authority over his wife, it would change *her* personal relationship with Christ. Upon marriage, her relationship with Christ would become corporate, with her husband as the go-between between her and Christ. Her husband's personal relationship with Christ would remain the same, but with the added responsibility of mediating for his wife. This is in opposition to what the apostle Paul says about Christ in 1 Timothy 2:5. Paul says there is "*one* mediator between God and man, the man Jesus Christ."

Protestants believe that Catholic priests cannot mediate between God and man, but they are willing to give husbands this divine power. If such a thing were possible, that would make him a god/mediator and his wife a lesser being than himself.

Yet complementarian men are falling for the temptation to "be like God" when they insist on becoming mediators between their wives and God. Remember that the serpent tempted Eve by saying "You will be like God..."

Marriage has become the new instrument of salvation

Bruce Ware explains how he believes marriage is the instrument of *women's* salvation. Bob Allen, then a reporter for ethicsdaily.com, quoted Ware when Ware spoke at a church in Denton, Texas:

> "Ware also touched on a verse from First Timothy saying that women "shall be saved in childbearing," by noting that the word translated as "saved" always refers to eternal salvation. "It means that a woman will demonstrate that she is in fact a Christian, that she has submitted to God's ways by affirming and embracing her God-designed identity as—for the most part, generally this is true—as wife and mother, rather than chafing against it, rather than bucking against it, rather than wanting to be a man, wanting to be in a man's position, wanting to teach and exercise authority over men," Ware said. "Rather than wanting that, she accepts and embraces who she is as woman, because she knows God and she knows his ways are right

and good, so she is marked as a Christian by her submission to God and in that her acceptance of God's design for her as a woman."[1]

Ware – this professor of Christian Theology! – repeats this bizarre theology on April 13, 2010, when he was interviewed by Nancy Leigh DeMoss for her radio show Revive Our Hearts in a segment called "Men and women in the church."

In those words, Ware changes salvation for married women and makes marriage her instrument of salvation. Ware's plan of salvation for women becomes one of works. It also makes men and women unequal in salvation because men do not have to make such a decision as Ware claims women have to make.

This contradicts their own teaching because being equal in salvation is one thing complementarians claim women have in common with men. However, from this statement by Ware, women do not even have that. How single women or widows attain salvation is not explained. Ware also did not explain how young female children come to God when they have no concept of their future adult desires.

Again, complementarians are in agreement with the Roman Catholic Church. On May 5, 2010, Benedict XVI said, "Marriage is truly an instrument of salvation, not only for married people but for the whole of society."[2]

Instead of outright saying husbands can save their families, complementarians have given marriages that role. If the wife submits, the family will be reflecting Christ and the church. This is found in the Danvers Statement Affirmation #6, "Redemption in Christ aims at removing the distortions introduced by the curse. In the family, husbands should forsake harsh or selfish leadership and grow in love and care for their wives; wives should forsake resistance to their husbands' authority and grow in willing, joyful submission to their husbands' leadership." As noted in "What the Danvers Statement Really Means" in Chapter 12, redemption in Christ has nothing to do with male/female relationships, and is instead, a healing of human relationships with God.

Men often fail the leadership role assigned them

The Council on Biblical Manhood and Womanhood would agree with the pastor who quoted 1 Peter 3:1 and then said, "In order for them (wives) to honor God, they must submit to their husbands." This statement makes husbands more important than God, because wives must first submit to their husbands. This leverage is being used to control complementarian women, making it required behavior in many Christian marriages.

Even when a wife submits, the husband often fails in the leadership role. The pastor who quoted 1 Peter 3:1 also said in his sermon that he knew of a husband who signed all the household checks because he thought that was his job as leader of the family, and that another husband gave his wife a list of chores to do each day.

This shows husbands are not born leaders and mistake micromanaging mundane household matters for real leadership. It is left to each husband to subjectively determine what it means to be a leader in his family, and he often chooses immature domination and neglects spiritual leadership altogether.

John Piper on husbands' sinful demands

John Piper gives an example in a presentation entitled, *Does a woman submit to abuse?*[3] of a husband asking his wife to engage in immoral sexual behavior. He says that if a husband asks his wife to engage in group sex, she cannot submit to him because she has a greater obligation to submit to Christ and this would not be pleasing to Christ. So she says something like "honey, I want so much to follow your leadership as God calls me to do that. It would be sweet for me if I could enjoy your leadership. But I can't go there."

Notice that there is no condemnation for a husband who would ask his wife to engage in group sex, but, instead, an explanation is issued of how she can continue to honor and obey such a man who would lead her into sin. He remains her leader even though he has just attempted to lead her into immorality.

Complementarians claim they do not want women to be doormats, but it is not these teachers of the law who are actually living in those marriages. If a husband wants his wife to be a doormat, she will be a doormat. That is what the submission doctrine is about—freedom and monarchy for husbands, but limits, servitude, obedience and bondage, if the husband so decrees, for wives.

If the husband in Piper's example decides his wife shall engage in group sex, she will engage in group sex. Even if she used Piper's syrupy words to excuse herself from participating in sin, if her husband believes he has the right to force her to submit to him in everything, she must comply or face the consequences. According to Bruce Ware, if the wife does not submit to her husband, it is understandable to complementarians (because men are sinners, Ware said) when the husband beats her for non-submission.

Marriage is not the reflection of Christ's relationship to the church

John Piper believes that marriages reflect Christ's relationship to the church with husbands representing Christ and wives representing the church. Piper explains marriage this way in *Piper's Notes— Marriage: A Matrix of Christian Hedonism*:[4]

"God did not create the union of Christ and the church after the pattern of human marriage; just the reverse, he created human marriage on the pattern of Christ's relation to the church. The mystery of Genesis 2:24 is that the marriage it describes is a parable or symbol of Christ's relation to his people...He patterned marriage very purposefully after the relationship between his Son and the church, which he planned from eternity. And therefore marriage is a mystery—It contains and conceals a meaning far greater than what we see on the outside. What God has joined together in marriage is to be a reflection of the union between the Son of God and his bride the church."

Piper is a complementarian and one of the founders of the Council on Biblical Manhood and Womanhood, and possibly one of the most-quoted preachers today. Although the above quote was written in 1983, the theology it presents is still the backbone of the teaching that currently subjugates women.

Piper says at the time of creation God decided that a human marriage would symbolize Christ and the church. He says that is what Genesis 2:24 means when it says a man will leave his father and mother, be united with his wife, and they will be one flesh. Piper believes this is a reference to Jesus being united with the church, His bride. Piper says this is the mystery Paul is speaking of when he says that marriage is a profound mystery (Ephesians 5:32).

According to Piper's rationale, Christ's relationship to the church was revealed in Genesis. However, this relationship is not mentioned in the Old Testament or in the New Testament Gospels. Piper says Paul revealed it in those letters to the people of Ephesus.

Marriages cannot reflect Christ and the church

Piper is saying that every marriage is a pattern of Christ's relation to the church, with "wives taking their cue from the church and husbands taking their special cue from Christ." Piper does not explain how a marriage of unbelievers reflects Christ and the church, or how a marriage where one spouse is a Christian and the other spouse is not reflects this relationship of Christ and the church. Piper also does not explain how singleness fits into this new holy concept of marriage, in light of 1 Corinthians 7:8 where the apostle Paul says that singleness is preferred.

The problem with both the CBMW's teaching and Piper's explanation is that they are not biblical. They have changed something very important about Christ and the church. Since the Reformation, Protestant Christians have taught that each person makes his or her own decision to follow Christ, which can be done independently of any church, and this is commonly called "accepting Christ as your personal savior," or to be expressed accurately, "personally accepting

Christ as your savior." When a person makes such a decision, that person becomes one of the "church body" with full privileges.

However, complementarians teach that the husband is between God and the wife, and now her acceptance into the Body of Christ comes with the requirement that she must submit to her husband, while her husband has no such requirements.

Piper says the marriage reflects Jesus and the church. A human marriage can be used as an illustration, but there is no way a human marriage can reflect Christ and the church. To reflect something means that it looks exactly like it, as in a mirror image. In his picture of marriage, husbands look like Christ and wives look like the church. When the image is forced to enact the real thing, it causes confusion and distortion because men and women cannot portray Christ and the church.

Bruce Ware, of similar persuasion as Piper, also says that marriages reflect Christ and the church. In his interview with Nancy Leigh DeMoss, he explains:

> "Then you have Christ and the Church. He devises and designs marriage to be a reflection of that great glorious reality of the Husband, the Groom, Christ and His bride, the Church. What a privilege it is to live out this expression, yes, of the gospel and of the God of the gospel and of the fruit of that gospel, the Church of Jesus Christ. What a privilege and what a glory."[5]

Neither Ware nor Piper has a basis for this interpretation. The bible does not specifically say the church is the bride of Christ. It is sometimes expressed that way, where Jesus is believed to be the bridegroom himself in Jesus' parables, but it is just as likely that he is not.[6] There is no reason for Jesus and his relationship to the church to compare to a sexual union between a man and a woman. Also, where Ware sees privilege and glory for husbands, many wives would not agree with that assessment.

Marriages have wrongly been given equal status with Christ and the church

In Jeremiah and Isaiah, God is called the husband, or Master in some translations, and he is chastising His rebellious and unfaithful children and He is calling them back to him.

The closest the bible comes to a marriage portraying the relationship between God and his people is the story of Hosea and Gomer, the prophet and his adulterous wife. Hosea 3:1, "The Lord said to me, 'Go, show your love to your wife again, though she is loved by another and is an adulteress. Love her as the Lord loves the Israelites, though they turn to other gods and love the sacred raisin cakes.'" Surely that is not the image of a marriage that Ware and Piper are talking about.

Giving husbands rulership over wives puts marriage on an equal status with Christ and the church. This changes the status quo. When Christianity began, Christ was the head of the church, with each individual responding to Christ directly. But now, through complementarian teaching, marriages are put on equal footing with Christ and the church, with wives being led by their husbands instead of by Christ.

This kind of marriage is a mockery. Who put marriages on equal footing with Christ? It crept in when no one was looking, and now there is a serpent at the door with an apple in its hand.

Mutual Submission between two equals makes a strong marriage

Strong marriages do not depend upon the husband standing on the back of his wife demanding submission. Mothers and fathers need to stand side-by-side in an equal partnership to raise their children, and then grow old together—as equals. They should both show Christ in their lives, including towards each other. Mutual submission between two equals is what makes a Christ-like marriage, as they love each other as they love themselves.

CHAPTER 16

Creating divine men by misinterpreting scripture

Considering the answer Jesus gave to John and James when they asked for the privilege to sit at his right hand side when he came into his kingdom (Mark 10:38), it is highly doubtful that husbands can stand-in for Christ here on earth. But standing in for Christ is exactly what they would be doing if husbands were given the privilege by God to be heads over women. Christ does not share his headship with human males.

The scariest scriptures, Ephesians 5:22-24

Ephesians 5:22-24 is often quoted by those who teach that women must submit to their husbands.

> "Wives, submit to your husbands as to the Lord. For the husband is the head of the wife as Christ is the head of the church, his body, of which he is the Savior. Now as the church submits to Christ, so also wives should submit to their husbands in everything."

Those who quote Ephesians 5:22-24 do not adhere to it. The Danvers Statement Concern #8 is "The increasing prevalence and acceptance of hermeneutical oddities devised to reinterpret apparently plain meanings of Biblical Texts," but even their writers back away from the plain meaning of this text.

The plain meaning of Ephesians 5:22-24 is:

- Wives, submit to your husbands as to the Lord. *The plain meaning would put husbands on equal footing with God.*
- The husband is the head of the wife as Christ is the head of the church. *The plain meaning gives husbands salvation rights, judgment rights, forgiveness ability, healing ability, miracles, obedience authority, to accept worship, to answer prayers, and the right to receive tithes.*
- The husband is the savior of the wife just like Christ is the Savior of the church. *The plain meaning makes husbands saviors of their wives. Why would the great I AM, share His salvation right with an earthly man?*
- The church submits to Christ. *The plain meaning makes husbands worthy of having wives submit to them.*
- Wives should submit to their husbands in everything. *The plain meaning makes man divine and infallible.*

Does any Christian believe that men can save their wives, and that wives should submit to their husbands in absolutely everything? Ask your pastor about this and he will begin to qualify this statement. It is qualified when they say that women should not follow their husbands into sin. It is qualified when they say a wife should not endure physical abuse. It is qualified when they make old age or infirmity of a husband an exception to allow wives to make decisions for their aged or infirm husbands.

Anyone who reads Ephesians 5:23 and insists that this scripture means that the husband literally has spiritual or physical charge over his wife, has made a golden idol and named it *husband*. To read this scripture that way gives man divinity and nullifies the whole Bible that proclaims only "One" God.

The plain meaning of this scripture is scary, yet it is quoted so casually that we have accepted the part we want to hear "that wives should submit to their husbands," and have ignored the significance of the remaining part of that sentence.

What does Ephesians 5:22-24 mean?

These new Christians wanted to understand who Jesus was. While explaining how Christ was the head of the church, and thus the head of the new Christians, Paul said in effect "the best way I can think of is to compare it to your marriage." That is clear in Ephesians 5:32 when Paul says "This is a profound mystery, but I am talking about Christ and the church," meaning that instead of it actually being a human marriage he is referring to, it is the relationship that Christ has with the church that he is talking about. That is a far cry from Paul making a human marriage the focus.

Then Paul says that even though he is talking about the church, their marriages are important too. "However, each one of you also must love his wife as he loves himself, and the wife must respect her husband." The Common English Bible translates it this way, "Marriage is a significant allegory, and I'm applying it to Christ and the church. In any case, as for you individually, each one of you should love his wife as himself, and wives should respect their husbands."

Is the husband the head of the wife like Christ is head of the church?

However, some will still say "I believe that the husband is the head of the wife like Christ is the head of the church." Paul says exactly that in Ephesians 5:23. We do not know what Paul or the translators meant when they said those words. We do know that Jesus' sacrificial death and resurrection made him head of the church. Complementarian husbands become heads of their wives at their wedding ceremonies with comparatively little sacrifice. The two are so dissimilar, with Christ giving his life while a husband obtains a wife, that it appears sacrilegious to make that comparison. It is more probable that Paul meant for the Ephesians to look at their own families where the husbands were already the heads, and then think of Jesus as being the head of his church family. To compare Jesus and husbands culturally in the First Century is no problem, but to make a biblical commandment for 21st century husbands to be in authority over their wives promotes men to the god-head.

Traditionally interpreted, those words create a contradiction in what Paul wrote in 1 Corinthians 11:3, "Now I want you to realize the head of every man is Christ, and the head of the woman is man, and the head of Christ is God," because Paul told the Ephesians that Christ is head of the church which is comprised of both men and women, whereas he told the Corinthians that Christ is the head of men only. But we know that Christ is the head of female Christians, too.

Jesus himself answers the question

The answer is found in the Gospels. Jesus affirmed that he was the head of women both before and after his death. He left women no room for doubt. Think back to Mary of Bethany who he allowed to sit at his feet and learn from the Master himself. Then remember the Gentile woman to whom Jesus revealed that he was to be the savior not only to the Jews, but to all people, which included her. Read again how Jesus revealed to the Samaritan woman that he was the Messiah. And finally, stand before the tomb where Jesus, in his resurrected body, made himself known to Mary before he told any man that he was alive. Jesus himself was telling women that he alone is their head, and there is no middle man between them.

These are powerful events that cannot be discounted. Jesus' ascension into heaven did not change those truths. Women are as important to our Lord on this side of the cross as they were on the other side.

Headship has no place in the Gospels. Jesus said, "You know that those who are regarded as rulers of the Gentiles lord it over them, and their high officials exercise authority over them. Not so with you. Instead, whoever wants to become great among you must be your servant, and whoever wants to be the first must be slave of all, for even the

Son of man did not come to be served, but to serve, and to give his life as a ransom for many" (Mark 10:42b-45).

Jesus did not say that men were heads of their wives, and he did not indicate that men would be elevated to headship after his resurrection. Since Jesus did not bind women before his resurrection to their husbands, there is no reason to believe that Jesus would bind women to their husbands after his resurrection.

Male headship contrary to everything Jesus said

In fact, male headship is contrary to everything Jesus said. The apostle Paul recognized this in his letter to the Galatians (3:26-28) where he wrote, "You are all sons of God through faith in Christ Jesus for all of you who were baptized into Christ have clothed yourselves with Christ. There is neither Jew nor Greek, slave nor free, male nor female, for you are all one in Christ."

Therefore, we are presented with three scriptural challenges to the doctrine of men being the heads of women: 1) It is contrary to Jesus' teaching and actions; 2) it makes men the vicars of Christ on earth if men are the head of women; 3) it removes Christ from headship over women; otherwise you have to believe that it takes two—one divine God and one earthly god—to be the head of one woman.

Complementarian teaching has harmed the Gospel

Scriptures used to support complementarian teaching have been studied and explained, and the meanings, it seems, depends upon who is speaking at the moment. One theologian says this and another says something else entirely different. This has distorted Jesus in the process, and has elevated marriage into something it was never intended to be. These scriptures have caused as much hurt and unhappiness as any other scriptures in the Bible, all because of the demand for a complementarian interpretation of what Paul is saying.

Pastors, bloggers, and theologians have produced untold words describing how women are to submit and behave. Seminary professors have taught courses, and books have been written on the subject of the subordination of women. Careers have been built upon it. This does not glorify God. This does not build up the body of Christ.

Teaching that women must submit to their husbands, without taking into consideration how the culture of that day impacted what methods Paul used to teach about God, does not do anything to further the gospel. Instead, this teaching has harmed the gospel, just as it has harmed women.

Christ gave himself for the church

The beauty of Christ being the head of the church has been lost. Imagine! Christ gave himself for the church. There is abundant grace in those words. There is love. There is meaning for our lives. There is a reason to learn about and feast upon the Word of God. There is a reason for becoming a pastor. There is a reason to teach children about Jesus. There is a reason to give money and hours of service to a church. There is a reason to get up and go to church every Sunday. There is a reason to feed the hungry and minister to others. There is a reason for dedicating your life to the service of God. Christ is head! Shout it out. Our reason for doing these things is for Christ!

Jesus gave his life for those who make up the church body. Christ is the head of women, too, and not as a secondary head, sharing headship with husbands. Paul said "If I speak in the tongues of men and of angels, but have not love, I am only a resounding gong or a clanging cymbal" (1 Corinthians 13:1). Ephesians chapters one through four are also "love" chapters—the love Christ has for the church which includes both men and women. It is not love that demands female submission to males, and it cannot be prettied up enough to make it so.

The joy of both men and women submitting to Christ for what he has done has been stolen from Him. Concentrating on wives submitting to their husbands has obscured the real message.

Marriage roles have become the overriding theme

Because so many denominations and pastors have accepted complementarianism, marriage roles have become an overriding theme and even focal point of Christianity, diminishing the gospel of Christ.

The family has taken on a much larger priority in doctrine than it has for 2000 years. Christianity is now focused on the family and is swamped with male headship conferences, books on male leadership, and blogs that promote the gloriousness of "joyful" wifely submission.

Marriages *are* important, but they are not specifically important to the gospel. The entire body of Christ is important to the gospel. In reality, a marriage is a unit that produces and nurtures children, but has little function to the outside world.

The church body, on the other hand, has a major responsibility to the outside world. A husband ruling over his wife and children does not reflect the gospel. It is the body of Christ that reflects the intent of the gospel by looking outward to the world through teaching and ministries.

The body of Christ demonstrates the love of God

The body of Christ demonstrates the love of God through its actions: feeding the hungry, caring for the ill, loving our neighbor, proclaiming salvation, and showing justice. This is the way the church functions as the body of Christ.

The church is to be the presence of Christ. "Now you are the body of Christ, and each one of you is a part of it. And God has placed in the church first of all apostles, second prophets, third teachers, then miracles, then gifts of healing, of helping, of guidance, and of different kinds of tongues" (1 Corinthians 12:27-28). The body of Christ serves God through being filled with God's spirit and using the gifts the Spirit gives to each Christian.

Instead of focusing on outreach, complementarian teaching focuses churches inwardly on man-decreed gender and marriage roles. This weakens the whole body of Christ, because it has become divided into male and female sections.

When the church, the body of Christ, is divided, it cannot reflect Christ's relationship to the church. Jesus said that if a house is divided against itself, it cannot stand (Mark 3:25). A marriage that has specific roles for each spouse to play is divided against itself; they are not working in partnership, nor are they working within their gifting. Male headship distorts marriage, misrepresents salvation for women, creates enmity between the genders, and divides the entire body of Christ.

CHAPTER 17

Eternal Son Subordination flawed theology

Not only has the relationship between God and his people been distorted, new theologies have crept in concerning the Trinity. The Eternal Son Subordination is an old discounted view which has become the prevailing new theology that has gained wide acceptance among complementarians.

Many pastors either teach that Christ is continually in submission to God, and that is why women have to be continually in submission to their husbands, or they ignore the teaching altogether but do not speak out against it. Either way, women suffer and pastors themselves suffer when they are not strong enough to stand up to this teaching, look it in the face, and call it for what it is. It is a sin against God.

Three-fold purpose in teaching Eternal Son Subordination

The Eternal Son Subordination teaching claims that since Jesus is eternally submissive to the Father, wives are to be submissive to their husbands. This theology has become essential to complementarians' teaching of marriage. Their purpose in defending the Eternal Son Subordination is three-fold: 1) to claim that since Jesus is eternally both submissive to, yet equal to, the Father, so also must wives maintain equality with their husbands while being forever subjected to their husbands; 2) to provide justification for denying women's call to pastoral ministry, service as deacons, or other leadership positions; 3) to establish and maintain power and authority for human males.

The falsehood of Eternal Son Subordination theology

The falsehood of Eternal Son Subordination misrepresents both God and husbands, misrepresents the relationship of the Father, Son, and Holy Spirit with one another, and misrepresents the relationship of the Father, Son, and Holy Spirit with women. Somehow a marriage of two people, husband and wife, is supposed to imitate the Trinity of three. It is a sin, pastors, to redefine God.

This Eternal Son Subordination, better expressed as Son-Eternally-Submissive-theology, is false, complicated, and quite convoluted. It was taught centuries ago, disproven, then reappeared around 1977 led by George W Knight III. The founding of the Council on Biblical Manhood and Womanhood was greatly influenced by Knight, and, as of the date of this writing, he is still a Council member.

Even though CBMW was heavily influenced by Knight, they did not include the Eternal Son Subordination theory in the Danvers Statement. However, this redefinition of the Trinity was resurrected sometime around the year 2000, after egalitarians pointed out that the New Testament did not back up complementarian claims about men and authority.

Complementarians sought a different approach, and found one in the discounted Eternal Son Subordination theory which allowed them to track back to Genesis where men and women are made in the image of God. If they could convince enough people that one Person in the Godhead submitted to the other, they could have their link to authority, thus giving husbands headship over wives. They have clung to the theory like a life raft.

If you accept the Eternal Son Subordination theory, it is best to close your eyes to the fact that now, instead of having one God, the Trinity has been made into three Gods, two of which are lesser—or four, when you recognize that husbands have now become part of the Godhead.

The doctrine of the Trinity has been redefined

Kevin Giles, Australian renowned Anglican priest, theologian, and author of *The Trinity and Subordination,* counters complementarian teaching with this statement,

> "To bolster support for this "great cause" (the permanent subordination of women), the doctrine of the Trinity has been redefined and reworded to give the weightiest theological support possible to the permanent subordination of women. Every evangelical who has written in support of the eternal subordination of the Son is committed to the permanent subordination of women in the church and the home. This agenda is what drives them to advocate the eternal subordination of the Son."[1]

Cindy Kunsman[2] wrote, "It's not enough to just slam women but complementarians are so motivated by the *woman problem,* they will put Jesus in a dress and make Him out to be the eternal slave—a special purpose God. The one Divine Person who actually had a physical body that was male is given the "role" that is synonymous with women. In that sense, they put him in a dress. Even on that level, what sense does this teaching make? The one man who was a man is likened by analogy to a woman. The one who is given the pre-eminence in all things is secondary in power. Why?"

She was referring to Bruce Ware and his teaching that Jesus is in eternal submission to the Father. This theology is used to explain why women must submit to their husbands. It is the theology that is being taught to young future preachers at Southern Baptist seminaries.

Ware explains a portion of the Eternal Son Subordination theory in *The Father the Son and the Holy Spirit the Trinity as theological foundation for family ministry,* "In addition, just as the husband's thoughtful and loving headship should reflect Christ's relationship to the church (Eph 5:25-27, 31-32), so the wife's glad-hearted and consistent submission should reflect the church's privilege of absolute submission before the lordship of the Messiah (Eph 5:24, 31-32). Therefore, the type of submission a wife is called to render to her husband is joyful and glad-hearted." He goes on to say, "Just as God calls all of us to submit to authority with whole heart and willing spirit, so this special calling and privilege is given to wives as a reflection of the triune relations within the Godhead."[3]

Ware's explanation reduces our Lord and Savior, Jesus Christ, to that of a slave to the Father (absolute submission), and demotes Christ. Complementarians who teach this theology keep getting confused about the wife's role. In this particular comment by Ware, the husband represents both Jesus and God, while the wife represents the church. Again, it is a mystery where the Holy Spirit fits into this triune relationship.

Confusing explanation of God's relationship to Christ

Mary Kassian, one of those members present at the CBMW meeting where the word complementarian was coined, confuses us even more about the Trinity with her definition, "A complementarian is a person who believes that God created male and female to reflect complementary truths about Jesus. That's the bottom-line meaning of the word. Complementarians believe that males were designed to shine the spotlight on Christ's relationship to the church (and the LORD God's relationship to Christ) in a way that females cannot, and that females were designed to shine the spotlight on the church's relationship to Christ (and Christ's relationship to the LORD God) in a way that males cannot."[4]

Their spotlight is out of focus because there are no scriptures to back up that concept, unless you accept the interpretation of 1 Corinthians 11:3 that the head of every male is Christ (removing Christ from being the head of females) and that males are the authority over women. But when you accept that interpretation, then you have accepted divinity for human males, and have placed husbands/males in the Godhead.

Ware and Kassian believe that authority always belongs to men, while women should delight in submission. This theology is found nowhere in the Gospels. Jesus does not make any mention of a husband's authority over his wife symbolizing anything about the Trinity. In fact, when Jesus speaks about marriage, it is usually about divorce.

False teaching is accepted and harms women

When something like the Eternal Son Subordination theory becomes accepted by leaders who should know the scriptures and who are looked upon as knowledgeable experts, many of their followers can be persuaded by what is said, even though they may have doubts at first.

That happened with the *Malleus Maleficarum*,[5] or the *Witch Hunter's Bible*, which is a work of absolute hatred against women. This book describes how women could naturally be more susceptible to practicing witchcraft because of their inherent weaknesses and sinful natures which they had because they were born female.

Even then, many in the Christian community such as scholars and theologians doubted that there were creatures such as witches, but they became silent because of the overwhelming influence of the Roman Catholic Church.

"The immediate, and lasting, popularity of the Malleus essentially silenced those voices. It made very real the threat of one being branded a heretic, simply by virtue of one's questioning of the existence of witches and, thus, the validity of the Inquisition. It set into the general Christian consciousness, for all time, a belief in the existence of witches as a real and valid threat to the Christian world. It is a belief which is held to this day....Estimates of the death toll during the Inquisition worldwide range from 600,000 to as high as 9,000,000 (over its 250 year long course); either is a chilling number when one realizes that nearly all of the accused were women, and consisted primarily of outcasts and other suspicious persons." (*Malleus Maleficarum*).

Similarly, the Eternal Son Subordination is believed because it is repeated so often. And it is repeated so often because complementarians need this false theory in order to keep women subordinated. In her book, *Woman this is WAR!*,[6] Jocelyn Andersen exposes complementarian motivation for defending this heretical theology by quoting Charles Stanley, a leading Southern Baptist pastor who supports the subordination of women. In his book, *A Man's Touch*,[7] he wrote, "If there is no submission within the Godhead, then there is no basis for complementarianism." Thus Stanley affirms Kevin Giles when Giles said complementarian's agenda for female subordination is what drives the Eternal Son Subordination theory.

Doctrinal error of Eternal Son Subordination

Wade Burleson, well-known Southern Baptist pastor of Emmanuel Baptist Church in Enid, Oklahoma, addressed the Eternal Son Subordination on June 16, 2015, in his blogpost titled "Eternal Subordination and the SBC divorce rate."[8]

"...Southern Baptist leaders have made the tragic error of believing that a husband should rule and a wife should be submissive because the Bible demands it...Truth be known, the Bible calls any desire to control and dominate--be it the husband or the wife—'the curse.' Southern Baptist Convention leaders have wrongly pushed for men to lord their authority over their wives, and called on wives to submit to the authority of their husbands because of a belief in and promotion of 'the eternal subordination of the Son.'"

Burleson finishes with this prediction,

"I predict we will see the divorce rate of Southern Baptists decline in the next few years, and it will not be because of cultural accommodation. It will be due to our new leaders of the Southern Baptist Convention laying aside the doctrinal error of eternal subordination."

However, for Burleson's prediction to come to pass, there must be new leaders who are *willing* to lay aside this flawed theology.

In researching for this book, the author has read many papers and writings which attempt to explain from the scriptures why women must submit to their husbands. Most of these are dogmatic and autocratic, and one day they too, like the *Witch Hunter's Bible,* will be declared works of misogyny.

CHAPTER 18

Sexualizing the Trinity

Even complementarians had to know their Eternal Son Subordination doctrine did not hold water, so they reached for another prop and found it. They borrowed from the sales industry to make Christianity sexy and hedonistic.

Listen to what else John Piper had to say in *Piper's Notes—Marriage: A Matrix of Christian Hedonism*.[1] If you think it is headed toward sex, then you are exactly right. Referencing the sexual relationship between married couples, Piper writes,

> "And Paul does not build a dam against the river of hedonism; he builds a channel for it. Husbands and wives recognize that in marriage you have become one flesh; therefore, if you live for your private pleasure (masturbation) at the expense of your spouse you are living against yourself and destroying your own highest joy. But if you devote yourself with all your heart to the holy joy of your spouse you will also be *living for your joy and making a marriage after the image of Christ and his church.*" (Italics added.)

To single out sex in a marriage and use it as an "image of Christ and his church" is unbiblical and indefensible. It encourages husbands to claim that the acting out of their lust fantasies is "making a marriage after the image of Christ and his church." There is a strong temptation to try to make the physical become spiritual, which the pastors discussed in this chapter attempt to do.

This new role-based instrument of salvation is becoming as much about sex as the Roman Catholic Church was about sex. Within 300 years after Christ, the new Roman Catholic Christians were dealing with sex—particularly the celibacy of the clergy. Today in our 20th and 21st century, it is Protestant clergy who are promoting sex and touting their sexual prowess.

Timothy Keller

Timothy Keller, pastor of a fundamentalist Presbyterian mega church, wrote in his book, *The Meaning of Marriage*,[2]

> "Sex leads us to words of adoration—It literally evokes shouts of joy and praise. Through the Bible, we know why this is true. John 17 tells us that from all eternity, the Father, Son, and Holy Spirit have been adoring and glorifying each other, living in high devotion to each other, pouring love and joy into one another's hearts continually (cf. John 1:18; 17:5, 21,24-25). Sex between a man and a woman points to the love between the Father and the Son (1 Corinthians 11:3). It is a reflection of the joyous self-giving and pleasure of love within the very life of the triune God. Sex is glorious not only because it reflects the joy of the Trinity but also because it points to the eternal delight of soul that we will have in heaven, in our loving relationships with God and one another."

Keller gives a strange sexual translation to 1 Corinthians 11:3, "Now I want you to realize that the head of every man is Christ, and the head of the woman is man, and the head of Christ is God," by saying that this scripture means that sex between a man and a woman points to the love between the Father and the Son. Keller also attempts to back up this sexual meaning by referencing the Book of John, but these scriptures do not validate what he claims they do, either.

The Council on Biblical Manhood and Womanhood's influence on Keller is borne out in his book when he quotes George W. Knight III from *Recovering Biblical Manhood and Womanhood*.[3] Keller quotes Knight as saying, "Paul saw that when God designed the original marriage, He already had Christ and the church in mind. This is one of God's great purposes in marriage: to picture the relationship between Christ and His redeemed people forever!"

To sum up Keller's paragraph quoted above, Keller is saying that when husbands and wives have sex, particularly when they climax, (when else would there be "shouts of joy?") they are emulating how the Father, Son, and Holy Spirit rejoice in each other.

Mary Kassian

If what Keller says about the sexual joy between the Father, Son, and Holy Spirit doesn't cause a queasy feeling, then this writer does not know what will. Unless it is what Mary Kassian, a friend of the Kellers, wrote in her blog post entitled, *More Necessities for God Glorifying Sex*, "If I cherish the true meaning of sex, I will be eager to engage in it in a God-honoring way. I will long to unite with my husband physically to symbolically honor my spiritual longing for Christ."[4]

This statement by Kassian has her committing adultery in the marriage bed against her husband or Christ, or both, because she is having sex with one man while thinking about another. However, complementarians such as Kassian and Keller justify this deviation because they have made husbands representatives of Christ.

John Piper

Piper said almost the same thing, "What God has joined together in marriage is to be a reflection of the union between the Son of God and his bride the church." This clears up the mystery of what Piper was talking about earlier. The 'union' between the Son of God and his bride the church, according to Piper and Keller, is sex. Just as sex supposedly points to the love between the Father and Son, now the bride (the church) is involved…if you believe what Piper and Keller are saying.

Kassian and Keller on sex and the Trinity

Mary Kassian spells it out in the blog post mentioned previously: "It means that male and female physically come together as husband and wife (in a covenant union), as perfect counterparts (the apex of complementarity), give the totality of who they are to one another (the apex of mutuality), and momentarily have their sense of "self" eclipsed by the ecstasy of a one flesh union (which is a physical fore-shadowing of the coming spiritual consummation between Christ and the Church)."[5]

Kassian says exactly the same thing Keller says when he said that when a husband and wife climax while having sex, they are emulating the joy the Father, Son, and Holy Spirit have in each other.

Salvation by faith has been replaced by the marital bed

They have made the marriage bed into God's grand design and demoted salvation by faith into a secondary design. But salvation for the church body was God's grand design, not the marriage bed. Pro-creation was part of God's grand design in marriage, and the Bible does not shy away from sex. However, God's command to be fruitful and multiply does not indicate that the sex act reflects God Himself. Sex is procreational and recreational, but it is not symbolic of the relationship of the Father, Son and Holy Spirit.

Ed Young, Jr.

The following pastor brought the marriage bed to the pulpit, literal-ly. Sexperiments is the brainchild of Ed Young, Jr., of The Fellowship Church in Dallas. This Southern Baptist male headship mega church, with multiple satellite campuses, allowed its pastor to hold what he called "sexperiments." In 2008 he put a bed where the pulpit should be, and then in 2012 he held a 24-hour bed-in on his church roof with his wife, Lisa. Young says that "it is time to bring God back in the bed and put the bed back in church."[6]

That sensationalism caused Young to fail in his obligation as a minister to his congregation. He allowed the congregation to indulge in voyeurism as they saw their pastor and his wife on the bed together. This is temple prostitution of the wife, even though they were fully clothed.

Young and his 'Fifty Shades of They'

Young continues his sex emphasis in 2015 with his latest book *Fifty Shades of They* (a play on the title wording of the pornographic *Fifty Shades of Grey)*. According to the promo: "His book *Fifty Shades of They* gives you fifty simple, yet profound insights that will help any relationship thrive, from friendships to business partnerships to marriages. Based on biblical standards and the teaching of Ed Young, this book is written for anyone who is looking to give new life to their relationships."

One wonders why a pastor would connect his book based on biblical standards to a pornographic book glorifying deviant sexual behaviors.

Jumping on the bed-wagon

It is not surprising, then, that another pastor has jumped on the bed-wagon. In February 2015, Pastor Darren Walter of Current Church in Katy, Texas, put a bed behind the pulpit and declared "Sex is God's idea."[7]

Well, yes, sex is God's idea. The problem, however, is that there is no mention of Jesus talking about the beauty of sex. And, in this writer's studies of the New Testament, there is no indication that the Apostle Paul or Timothy glorified sex in a marriage. Certainly they never would have put a bed right up front and center. In the bible (Song of Songs), Solomon glorifies married and unmarried sexual desires; but then we must remember, Solomon had hundreds of wives and concubines and hardly seems the proper person to emulate in Christian marriage.

When a bed is put on stage, many men looking on will be picturing the pastor and his wife, the other staff, and other women in the congregation, having sex. The nature of humans is such that men in the congregation are not just thinking of having sex with their own wives, but are taking advantage of the pastor's endorsement to imagine having sex with any woman within sight. Perhaps many of the women in the congregation will be eyeing the males.

How can a pastor promote such adulterous thoughts and still believe that he is leading his congregation to honor "God-given sex?" This is damaging to the men in the congregation and makes women sex objects. It is damaging to young boys and young girls.

Sexually explicit pastor, Mark Driscoll

Another pastor, Mark Driscoll, formerly of now defunct Mars Hill Church, a nondenominational male headship mega church with multiple satellite campuses, was also heavily into sex sermons and books. He came under scrutiny in October 2014 with the accusation of plagiarism, of being a bully, and his leadership style which included inappropriate sexual content in his sermons. His apparent obsession with sex as evidenced in his sermons and books upset many Christians. However, less than six months after his resignation, Driscoll made a comeback and was being invited to speak and appear at Christian conferences.[8] An irony is that the former Mars Hill Church has been sold to an egalitarian congregation called Quest Church.

Because Mark Driscoll is attempting to reinstate his ministries,[9] it is appropriate to discuss what he taught on his previous website because many of his followers found nothing wrong with his message. This writer does, however.

Driscoll frequently had Bruce Ware lecture at his church on marriage and the Trinity using the Eternal Son Subordination theory. Driscoll writes about his own marriage in a book he wrote with his wife, Grace, called *Real Marriage* (2012).[10] His book borders on pornography, and his supporters have a hard time defending it. Denny Burk, who is on the staff of CBMW as a journalist, writes, "I question the wisdom of addressing sexual topics in such explicit detail."[11]

Driscoll ratted on his wife when he told about a sexual relationship she had before he married her. He said that he would not have married her if he had known about it beforehand. This was much like when Adam ratted out on Eve when he said "this woman you put here with me gave me some of the fruit, and I ate it." The *loving your wife* part of male headship just fell by the wayside.

Mark Driscoll on wives and the devil

In 2013, on his website, Driscoll paraphrased I Timothy 2:15 this way, "Yet she will escape [from Satan's attack] through childbearing [and wifely roles]—if they continue in faith and love and holiness, with self-control." Driscoll then goes on with his explanation of I Timothy 2:15 to show how he comes up with his particular understanding of that scripture. "Paul's exhortation is simple: we were created to operate in a certain order. Jesus is the head, the husband under him, and the wife and children under him. This is not devaluing; it is protection. When this order is broken—when a wife tries to take authority sinfully or the husband refuses to accept it lovingly—*Satan is given an opportunity to attack the husband and wife,*"[12] (italics added).

In this quote, Driscoll *is* devaluing women by classifying the wife as equal with the children, with both wife and child submitting to the father. This makes the wife the oldest female child—with bedroom responsibilities.

This instrument-of-salvation marriage hinges upon wives submitting to their husbands and husbands taking authority over their wives. Driscoll says when wives take authority away from their husbands, it is a sin. However, a husband's refusal to provide "loving" headship, is not treated as sin.

According to Driscoll, a husband having authority over his wife, and the wife submitting, will not allow Satan in. It is in this way that

Driscoll declares role-played marriage to be the instrument of both salvation and protection from Satan.

Driscoll and the Council on Biblical Manhood and Womanhood in agreement on women and the devil

The Council on Biblical Manhood and Womanhood says the same thing on their website (Missions and Vision) that Driscoll says:

> "If families do not structure their homes properly, in disobedience to the teachings of Ephesians 5, 1 Peter 3, and Colossians 3, then they will not have the proper foundation from which to withstand the temptations of the devil and the various onslaughts of the world. This hinders the sanctification of married couples and also introduces confusion about basic parenting issues such as raising masculine sons and feminine daughters." (CBMW.org)

Shockingly, this is the same language found in the *Malleus Maleficarum* (The Witch Hunter's Bible). Wikipedia quotes Michael Bailey (*Battling Demons*, 2003, University Press):

> "The text argues that women are more susceptible to demonic temptations through the manifold weaknesses of their gender. It was believed that they were weaker in faith and more carnal than men. Michael Bailey claims that most of the women accused as witches had strong personalities and were known to defy convention by overstepping the lines of proper female decorum."

Women consorting with the devil was a strong belief in the Middle Ages, and it has not disappeared in Christian circles as is seen in the statement by the Council on Biblical Manhood and Womanhood. If a woman becomes too strong, usurping the authority of the husband, she is guilty of inviting the devil into the home, according to them.

Driscoll and the Council on Biblical Manhood and Womanhood believe that when wives submit themselves to their husbands, this enables families to withstand the devil's temptations and the onslaughts of the world. If you believe that is the gospel, then you need to find yourself a real Bible.

Pastors must return to the Gospel

Complementarian Protestants are headed toward a Dark Ages of Christianity unless they open their eyes to these false teachers. Pastors must return to the Gospel. What they do in their bedrooms is not for others to view or read about. Certainly the apostle Paul would not recommend that pastors engage in public bedroom confessions.

As is shown throughout this book, Jesus was not concerned about raising masculine sons and feminine daughters, nor was he concerned with wives submitting themselves to their husbands, and neither did he indicate that husbands were strong enough to keep Satan from entering into a family.

Emphasis must be taken off marriage and husbands' authority and refocused on Christ as being the head of the church. The falling away of the church should be the primary concern instead of some role being enacted every time a husband and wife go to bed. Too many pastors have taken the lead from Piper in prioritizing marriage and making it an instrument of salvation and sexualizing the Trinity.

CHAPTER 19

How churches teach
male headship

Arguing for women's equality, this writer wrote to a minister friend concerning male headship, and this was his reply: "I really think that God intended for every man to be the spiritual leader of his family. He is to provide an example of Christ to his wife and children that would cause them to see and want Christ in their life. When a man does that, his wife will be more than happy to allow him to lead the family."

The problem with that pastor's statement is that 1 Peter 3:1 says it is the wives who might lead their husbands to the Lord by their actions. Instead of giving the leadership role to husbands, the scriptures actually say that it is both men and women who can be the spiritual leaders and who can lead the other one to Christ by example, as is also found in 1 Corinthians 7:15-16. These passages teach that both husbands and wives can lead, and they make no case for male leadership.

In light of the teachings of Christ, and all of the New Testament, it is a sin against God to teach that the female of his creation is of lesser quality than the male. Churches teach this travesty that women's bodies are not of good enough quality—spiritual or physical—and that is why they will not allow women to be pastors or deacons. That is why they teach that women must have males in leadership over them. The

Danvers Statement Affirmation #1 says it plainly: "Both Adam and Eve were created in God's image, equal before God as *persons* and distinct in their manhood and womanhood."

It is the physical male body

If men and women are equal in their persons, and one gender has been given authority over the other, the only determining factor as to who has the superior role is the physical body.

Their reasoning is that God chose men for decision-making roles in the church and home, and their ability to lead comes from the fact that their *body* is male – not that their brain is male. If that is not the case, then why are women immediately rejected from leadership without ever determining what qualifications and spiritual gifts they may have? A female body, no matter what level of education or experience the woman has, or the depth of her spirituality, is seen as a poor or unacceptable substitute for a male. Some question if a woman can even be put into ministerial service if no man is around to do the job. Again, neither qualification nor the urgent need for a minister has anything to do with determining whether or not a woman can lead.

Again, we look to Bruce Ware when he told Nancy Leigh DeMoss in an interview that was previously mentioned:

> "Complementarians believe women by virtue of their being women regardless of their gifting, regardless of their training, their character, all of those things put together, *would not qualify her to pastor a church simply because she is a woman.*"(italics added for emphasis).

It is the male physical anatomy that is the determining factor, plain and simple.

Adoration of the male body

It should come as no surprise that John Piper, who helped write the Danvers Statement, and is a founding member of the Council on Biblical Manhood and Womanhood, said that God intended Christianity to have a masculine feel. That is a peculiar statement for a Christ-follower to make, but his explanation is even stranger. He said that the Sunday morning worship service is to be primarily led by males, with "women loving it, they're radiant, they're intelligent, they're under-standing, they're processing, they're interacting."

Piper says that when anyone walks into church on Sunday morn-ing, the room is full and radiating with this male energy, and that is how women are responding. Then they hear a word from God, spoken by a male pastor. Piper goes on to say that within this church commu-nity men have some qualities that are definitely associated with being feminine and that women have some qualities that are definitely mas-culine.[2]

Direct opposition to what Jesus taught

What Piper says is in direct opposition to what Jesus taught. Jesus taught that people make decisions in their hearts as to how they choose to obey and serve God. Jesus said, "I tell you, no! But unless you repent, you too will all perish" (Luke 13:3).

Repentance comes from the heart and mind, not from an emotional response to testosterone in a worship service. Most evangelical church worship services end with a call to accept Christ as savior and that decision should be from the heart, and not from emotions that are stirred up by a display of male leadership. This leaves no room for applying gender roles within a worship service in order to get a re-sponse.

So, while Piper's statement comes as no surprise, it is a statement made because he felt he needed to justify an all male led worship ser-vice.

When denominations deny women the privilege of preaching, pas-toring, or serving as deacons or elders, it is because they believe women cannot hold those positions because they are female. They support this teaching with nonsense about the hormonal effect on women's emotions, and the effect on a woman's body during men-

142 • SHIRLEY TAYLOR

struation, which takes us back to the 1950s when girls were not allowed to participate in sports or wash their hair during that time of the
month. Preposterously, they ignore that it is male testosterone that has
been the cause of much violence, including murders, continual wars,
as well as the physical battering of women. Apparently from the previous statement by Piper, testosterone is what both men and women
respond to in a worship service.

Thus Piper proves the point. It is not qualifications, masculinity or
femininity, nor spirituality that makes men desirable as leaders in the
church. It is the male body. What is not explained is how this adoration of the male body translates into the worship of God.

Because males are seen leading the worship service each Sunday
morning, congregations have become accustomed to women being in
the background and accept this as normal. They do not realize this
conditioning has led them into sin by keeping women from visible
leadership positions. It is a sin to decide that women are not spiritually
or physically qualified for church and home leadership just because
they are female.

Pastors make the decision to enforce male authority

The Director of Missions in a Baptist association said pastors in his
association had already made their decisions and were not going to
change their minds. Those pastors had persuaded their churches to
accept the Baptist Faith and Message 2000, with the majority of members having only a slight idea of what they had signed. Other groups
pushed for their members to accept the Danvers Statement composed
by the Council on Biblical Manhood and Womanhood.

One Baptist denominational secretary said the Bible does not say
women are inferior and churches do not teach that they are. She has
not considered her own church by-laws which deny women equality,
or the Danvers Statement that tells her she is limited to certain roles
because she is a woman, or the Baptist Faith and Message 2000 that
tells her she must submit graciously to her husband.

This makes women inferior

Churches *do* teach that women are inferior. Every time a parent takes a son or a daughter inside a complementarian church, the message given is that the son is superior to the daughter and the daughter is inferior to her brother. A baptized boy, who may be only nine years old, has full privileges of membership that full grown female members do not have. *If you do not think that makes a woman inferior, then you need to rethink your definition of inferior.*

Rather than listening to God, all too often, pastors listen to men who create new theologies to justify silencing women and continually seek to "put women in their place." For example, a guest preacher at an Assembly of God mega church in Springfield, Missouri, told the congregation, "Women, you know you are under the authority of your husbands, but I don't have time to preach on that today."

With those words, he informed over one thousand women of their inferior positions and that they were to submit to their husbands just because he wanted to get that point across. What he did not realize was that he had just diminished God with those words and farmed out women to their husbands.

These pastors know the scriptures. They should also know the whole theme of the Bible, and they should have enough love of Christ in them to rightly discern between the scriptures that tell women to be silent in church, the scriptures that tell women to prophesy in church, and the scriptures that report how, with Paul's blessing, women were leaders in the churches. They should also be looking at the four Gospels and to Jesus for their direction.

How can anyone find justification for "allowing" or not allowing women to serve God as they are called?

Godly husbands should be on their knees begging for equality for their wives and daughters. Proponents of male headship say they would give up their lives for their wives like Christ did for the church, but these same men will not allow their wives the full expression of salvation given to them by the One who *did* die for them.

What can women do in church?

In a complementarian church, women are involved in the ministries of the church as paid staff and volunteers. Paid staff includes administrative assistants, directors of women and children's ministries and music; unpaid volunteers spend untold hours in church-sponsored ministries. However, the office as pastor to adult men is reserved for men, as are unpaid volunteer positions such as elders and deacons.

Wayne Grudem, the leading founder of the Council on Biblical Manhood and Womanhood, has come up with *Which Roles Should Be Open to Women*[3] which is a list of things that men can do and what women are restricted from doing regarding vocational and volunteer work in churches and denominational entities. There are about 80 things (some are duplications) on his three lists.

The title of List 3 is *Areas of public visibility or recognition.* Grudem's wording is confusing and it helps to keep in mind that he is headed toward only one declaration in this list, and that declaration is that women cannot be ordained as pastors.

This is how Grudem's List 3 is worded, *Which activities should be restricted to men? (listed in order of greatest to least public visibility or recognition in a local congregation).* Directly beneath that question is another heading, *Public recognition that should be restricted to men.* Only one thing is listed and that is *Ordination as pastor (member of the clergy) in a denomination.* With all of Grudem's headings, he finally gets to what he wanted to say in the first place, and that is that *women cannot be pastors.*

It is not known how many churches actually refer to Grudem's list when they are trying to fill volunteer vacancies or when seeking people for low salaried positions. But while they will compromise on many of the positions on Grudem's lists, they will not compromise on List 3 which forbids women to be pastors.

John Piper's list of what is Biblically appropriate

John Piper's list[4] of what is "Biblically appropriate" for Christian women is demeaning to huge groups of people. Since he believes that women cannot teach nor have authority over men, then it appears that those to whom women can teach, are less valuable people. It is worth noting that in his list 'women' is a stand-alone group, positioned between abused children and runaways. Piper's list is found in his book *Recovering Biblical Manhood and Womanhood: A Response to Evangelical Feminism*, (page 48). This is how Piper's list begins:

> "Ministries to the handicapped, hearing impaired, blind, lame, retarded, ministries to the sick, hospice care-cancer, AIDS, etc., community health, ministries to the socially estranged, emotionally impaired, recovering alcoholics, recovering drug-users, escaping prostitutes, abused children, women, runaways, problem children, orphans, prison ministries, women's prisons, families of prisoners, and rehabilitation to society, etc."

From the list, we see that Piper allows women to teach males who have societal, physical or mental problems. Piper makes no allowance for women to teach men who are sitting in the church pew on Sunday morning, even though, they, too, might have such problems.

Female restrictions are common knowledge

One church allows women to sing as long as they are facing the pulpit but not if they turn their heads to the side, because they cannot sing the gospel to a person sitting next to them. One church will not allow a woman to teach a boy after he has been baptized, even if he is only nine years old. Another church will not teach young girls how to be a verbal witness for the gospel, even though they will teach young boys this skill. One church would not allow a woman to stand behind the pulpit to give a eulogy of her father at his funeral.

Many churches will not allow a woman to teach a man in a Sunday school class unless the teacher's husband is also in the room to be her "covering" authority. This so-called "covering" has no biblical basis because the very act would mean that a husband can supersede the scriptures.

To a large degree, pastors determine what women are allowed to do in their churches. One city church had a woman staff member with a seminary degree. She was allowed behind the pulpit on Sunday morning to welcome guests and members to the church and to say a prayer. When the pastor of that church retired, she was moved aside. The church began asking a husband and wife duo to stand behind the pulpit to welcome guests, after which the man prayed. Suddenly the woman had to have the *covering* of her husband's authority—which they believe he has because he was born male—in order to stand behind the pulpit.

Church restrictions are often not written down but are common knowledge among church members. In the case of the woman who was removed from praying in public, many of the members may not have agreed with what was happening, but few said so, because it was common knowledge that women should not have been behind the pulpit in the first place. Those rules can change with each pastor without any by-laws ever reflecting those changes. Some pastors are strict in their adherence to rules of what women can and cannot do. Others are not as strict, even though they are each following the same written rules. Nevertheless, these churches will not remove written restrictions against women, nor will they speak up against such teaching in their peer groups.

Matthew 23 says, "The teachers of the law and the Pharisees sit in Moses' seat. So you must obey them and do everything they tell you. But do not do what they do, for they do not practice what they preach. They tie up heavy loads and put them on men's shoulders, but they themselves are not willing to lift a finger to move them."

Fences are for animals, not wives

Mary Kassian, a member of the CBMW, describes those limits in the church and home as being that of a big beautiful field with a fence around it. In *Boundaries are for your freedom*[5] she advises women not to press their noses up against the fence desiring something they cannot have. However, Kassian's description is hard to swallow, because it is animals that need to be penned up behind a fence—not wives.

Churches will not give women the dignity of equality

Women are heavily involved in volunteer positions and in decision-making in many churches as we have seen in this chapter. However, their paid and volunteer work is restricted because of the limitations placed upon them by what has been termed "women's roles." It is a fact that churches cannot function without the work and influence of women. By their actions, many churches recognize that, but will not give women the dignity of equality.

Far too much time is wasted on what women can and cannot do in churches. There are seven billion people in the world, most needing to hear the gospel, and Christians tie themselves in knots trying to keep women from standing behind a pulpit!

CHAPTER 20

Pastors' responsibility to the whole congregation

Pastors are hesitant to speak out for women's equality. They do not want to rock the boat. They fear money leaving their church as much as they fear people leaving. They fear angry voices being raised against them, plus they face the loss of fellowship with other pastors of their denomination or pastors of similar faiths.

Gerald Ford, a Christian counselor, speaks about churches that are afraid they will lose half their church members if the women's equality discussion begins. Ford says, "This half of their church that is left will perhaps be a whole half since the church is beginning to recognize both halves. Better yet, the church is beginning to realize that in Christ there is neither male nor female. A church willing to die for Christ is more Christ-like than the one whose main goal is self-preservation."

The conversation must begin

At some point the conversation will have to happen. Pastors are deciding now if they want to continue to be part of the problem holding back women's equality or if they want to follow Christ and be part of the solution.

A friend's pastor said that strife in a church was the worst possible thing, and God does not like strife in the church. He said that bringing up women's equality would cause strife. He also claimed that women are not unhappy—maybe a little group is, but most women are just fine with it. The friend asked "Why don't those women who are dissatisfied leave and find a church that believes like they do?"

That friend's pastor is putting women on notice to keep quiet. Remaining silent is what women have always done. The pastor is aware that the loudest voices in a church are those who are against the idea of women serving as deacons, elders, and pastors. The pastor either fears or agrees with the loudest voices that will be raised when the church mentions changing the by-laws to let women serve the Lord's Supper. The church by-laws are the cold heart of the church because they are the written word of what women can and cannot do.

The pastor knows he can count on those who want an equal voice and presence for women to either remain silent or quietly leave.

Encouraging women to leave the church is a short term solution. Denying women equality because they were born female is a sin against the new creation that the apostle Paul speaks about in 2 Corinthians 5:17, "Therefore, if anyone is in Christ, the new creation has come: the old has gone, the new is here!" When women's equality is denied, sin is still in the church, and the pastor must deal with that sin. The pastor must also deal with his own sin in perpetuating gender division.

Why do women have a new law and men do not?

In Galatians 5:7-12, Paul chides Christians for allowing someone to come in and stir them up by telling them they have to obey the law again, particularly in regards to circumcision. Paul reminds them that when they teach the old law, they have ignored the cross of Jesus. You can sense Paul's frustration when he blurted out, in verse 12, "I wish they would go the whole way and emasculate themselves!" Today Paul would say, "cut it all off!" You get the picture. Women are not circumcised, but because they have a female body, they have been made to wear the cloak of oppression. Putting restrictions upon women and forcing them to obey laws that have nothing to with the gospel makes Christ "die for nothing" (Galatians 2:21b).

Gender inclusivity movement in the Church of Christ

One Church of Christ minister said that the issue of gender inclusivity had arisen in his church. Hoping his members would see the light, he held Bible classes on the subject. His church was evenly divided between those who thought women should have greater visibility in the church through worship and leadership and those who thought the scriptures taught that women were to remain silent and have no voice in spiritual or business matters of the church.

Since men were the leaders and the ones who would vote on any change the church made, it was an all-male group. He said that when the classes ended, those in the group who did not want women's equality still did not want it, and those who did, still wanted women to be included in full service. Their attitudes remained the same. No change. Also no change in the way the church dealt with women's equality, even though about half of the men felt that women should be treated equally in the church. Because the loudest and most insistent voices were those against women's inclusivity, those who were originally for it kept quiet in order to keep the peace. To nobody's surprise, the loudest voices won again.

Another Church of Christ church recently reported that they could be listed under the egalitarian heading, but not without cost. The church previously had over 400 congregants, but now has only 200 or so remaining. The members who left did so because the church was deciding for gender inclusivity, and they would not put up with it. However, those same people did not realize that those who remained in the congregation had been "putting up with" a denial of gender equality for years and had not caused a problem in the church. Again, it was not those who desired women's equality who caused problems, but those who sought to deny women, who caused dissension in a church.

In 2014 another very large Church of Christ church led the discussion on allowing more women in leadership positions. However, this church said at the beginning of their discussions they would not address the possibility of women preachers.

Apparently that was necessary because when it came time to vote, the church voted to allow women limited leadership positions, whereas the discussion would possibly have bogged down and resulted in a loss for all women if 'women preachers' had not been removed from the table. That is a slap in women's faces, however, because they still held preaching and pastoring as the big prize that women could not attain because of their gender.

Traditions cause opposition to change

The administrative assistant in a moderate Baptist church in Texas said her church had spent several years discussing whether women could be deacons. "But," she said, "when it came down to a vote, it almost failed." The vote passed, but not by much. Regardless of all the scripture and explanation they had read, the emotional impact and traditions of being a Baptist were almost too much for that church to accept women deacons.

That attitude must change because the scriptures do not support gender discrimination in any form or fashion.

At another Baptist church, some members hinted they possibly would be interested in beginning discussions about allowing women to be deacons in their church. This caused several families to leave the church. The pastor had to reassure the remaining members that they would not discuss women's equality again. The sad thing is the pastor himself was for women's equality. This pastor had to compromise his own conviction, that God considers women as qualified and called for leadership in the church, in order to keep the peace in his church. Again, the strife did not come from those who wanted equality but from those who wanted to keep women from equality.

When this writer first began her ministry of promoting women's equality, she received a letter that said, "I don't have a beef now;

however, if this issue is ever confronted in our local church, I will have a beef and predict it will be very divisive." Just as predicted, when the issue came up in her church, it was divisive, and that divisiveness was not caused by those who wanted equality.

The harvest is plentiful, but only men are allowed in the field

In Paul's letter to the Ephesians (2:12-13), he welcomed the new Gentile Christians into the faith, "Remember that at that time you were separate from Christ, excluded from citizenship in Israel and foreigners to the covenants of the promise, without hope and without God in the world. But now in Christ Jesus you who once were far away have been brought near through the blood of Christ." Those words are still critical today. We, too, should be welcoming new converts. However, church membership is declining.

Pastors must speak out for women's equality in the church because of the great falling away from the gospel that has already begun in their churches. When asked to identify with a religious belief system, more and more people are checking the box that says "none." Thus a new name "Nones" has been created. That is a sad indictment against churches.

Remember, Paul began his letter to the Ephesians with Christ's love for his people. Paul's letter to the Galatians, in chapter 3 verses 26-29, also expresses Christ's love for his church. He wrote, "You are all sons of God through faith in Christ Jesus. For all of you who were baptized into Christ have clothed yourselves with Christ. There is neither Jew nor Greek, slave nor free, male nor female, for you are all one in Christ Jesus. If you belong to Christ, then you are Abraham's seed, and heirs according to the promise."

The focus on getting men back into church

While churches are busy with building programs or are wrapped up in self-preservation mode, the people who they hoped to connect with have already left. Pastors scratch their heads and wonder what is happening and plan for more "he-man" programs to catch the attention of men. Power lunches are instituted to appeal to men. Big Day Events[1] and Wild Game Events[2] are promoted to attract more men into church.

With the focus on getting men to come into the door, the church has lost focus on the women who are walking out the door and taking the kids with them.

In recent years we have seen a huge decline of women in professional occupations attending church. This is echoed by Sandra Crawford Williamson who said in her blog "Why are Working Women Starting to Unplug from Their Churches?"[3] Williamson said, "We need to figure out quickly how to recognize, encourage, and spiritually lead these (professional) women. Barna and others say as many as 27% of professional Christian women are starting to choose to unplug from church all together." As she points out, these are women who have been attending church, and now the church no longer 'fits' because the church provides no teaching with which they can identify. You can be assured these women are not looking for spiritual motivation by Wild Game Events or washed-up sports figures with three divorces behind them, which is what some of these churches offer.

The "Nones" previously mentioned say they still pray to God and God is important in their lives, but these parents will not necessarily teach their children to pray, and the next generation will not be supporting the mega churches that demand female submission. They will be absent in both city and country churches that are still pushing legalistic laws against women. A church is hypocritical when it binds its women while the men go free, and this hypocrisy is not lost to the younger generation.

Pastors have a decision to make

Many individuals within churches are coming to the conclusion that it is time for their churches to change. Will you listen to those voices calling out for equality for women in your congregation, or will you force them to go elsewhere?

Luke 10:2 says "The harvest is plentiful, but the workers are few. Ask the Lord of the harvest therefore to send out workers into his harvest field." Women are ready to go. They love the Lord and His Word; they are educated, trained, and ready to go out into the field. It is the church that is turning these workers away because they care more for legalism than they care for people.

History has shown that churches and denominations have often been on the wrong side and now they are again. Pastors of all denominations and faith groups have a decision to make. History is being made now. Pastors, you have a great responsibility. How will you be remembered? Will your church be recognized as one who opened its doors to women deacons and women pastors, or will your church be remembered as closing its doors to over one-half of God's people? Can the religious papers, blogs, and books that you have written be compared to the condemnation of women found in the *Witch Hunter's Bible?*

What pastors can do for their congregations

What can pastors do without causing strife in their churches? There will be a struggle. Jesus does not promise us life without struggle. Change does not come about easily, but the wait for Christian women's equality has been far too long. There are enough books and blogs written and sermons preached about the authority of men over women that everyone in your church is likely aware of at least some of the terminology, and has an opinion on it based upon something they have heard or read. Pastors would be surprised to know how many men and women sitting in their churches are ready for equality.

You must prepare yourself. You can do this any way you choose, but you must begin with something. A simple plan is "Commit to 5," a plan that will give direction and lead to deeper understanding of this subject. Pastor, you are in charge, and the greater responsibility is yours. Choose one or more of the points below and encourage others to join you in committing to do them for five months. At the end of that time, look for a difference in the way your congregation responds to the subject of women's equality.

Commit to 5 for pastors

- Pray daily for women's equality
- Learn more about women's equality by reading articles and books supporting egalitarian gender equality and place these books in your church library. A good resource for books and free articles on gender equality is Christians for Biblical Equality at www.cbeinternational.org.
- Attend a conference such as those hosted by Christians for Biblical Equality. Engage in an egalitarian book discussion group or internet forum with other pastors who are open to learning about women's equality.
- Make one change in the way you engage your congregation in worship. Allow women to read scripture from the pulpit and pray publicly in worship. Ask women from what activity or office they feel excluded in your church simply because they are women.
- Tell your peers what you and your church are doing to bring about women's equality. This is important and will encourage others who are wavering.

Make it count! Put actions to your words

Pastors can start with their local associations or districts and form connections with other pastors who realize, or who are beginning to realize, that they are not treating over one half of their congregations as Jesus taught. Remember what Jesus said, "Love the Lord your God with all your heart and with all your soul and with all your mind. This is the first and greatest commandment. And the second is like it: Love your neighbor as yourself."

After approaching your local association or district about changing their teaching, move on to the next level. Put on your armor and head to the national convention. Denominations are structured in many different ways. Most have larger councils or leadership groups that help shape the future of the denominations. If they do not have that, then approach the seminary where your pastors are taught. You should do that anyway. You have a voice. Your voice has been drowned out by those who yell the loudest, and who are the most prolific in their blogging and writing and speaking against women's equality.

Most church members are intelligent and educated. Scripture is inspired and comes from God according to 2 Timothy 3:16, but there is no scripture that says that all translations are inspired by God. All Bibles today are translations, and denominations have their favorite translations. The original manuscripts were lost. That is not to say translators were not inspired by God, but translators are human, prone to their own bias, and that is why pastors and congregations need to read several different translations to compare scripture. For instance, when women are told to keep silent in 1 Corinthians 14:34-35, Paul seems to be contradicting what he said in Chapter 11 about how women can pray and prophesy (preach). If women can preach in Chapter 11, what changed so they are barred from preaching in Chapter 14? Restore the hunger to know what God meant, not what some people have said God wants.

Pastors of nondenominational churches should look for a local group of like-minded pastors and begin to speak up. All pastors have a great responsibility. That responsibility extends to both halves of the congregation, not just to those members who threaten to leave the church if a woman is ordained as a deacon or elder, or is allowed to preach, but also to those members who desire a shared ministry in their church.

Pastors must be careful in their conversation about women

Pastors and denominations have a responsibility to be careful about what they promote as family values to their members. In the fall of 2012, many churches of a major denomination that has women pastors led a series on the family. Because they have women ministers you would expect them to be firmly grounded in their stance regarding equality for women.

However, that was not the case. One of their suggested readings was *The Meaning of Marriage* by Timothy Keller, a book that is totally complementarian and which has already been mentioned in Chapter 18 under the heading "Sexualizing the Trinity." This book expounds on the joy women have in being secondary to husbands in the home and in the church.

Any teaching that tells women that they must submit to their husbands without mutual submission, also teaches that women cannot have pastoral authority over men. Whether by design or carelessness in research, this denomination that already has women pastors promoted an author who firmly believes and teaches that women have no place behind the pulpit.

Pastors must be careful which pastors they quote in their sermons. If the congregation hears quotes from John Piper, Timothy Keller, or other complementarians, it is likely they will consider these pastors approved by their pastor. Then when they read books on male headship by these pastors (it is hard to find books on equality), it will appear to them as reasonable since their pastor has often quoted these people.

Churches must be egalitarian

Do not be afraid of the subject of equality for Christian women. The conversation must begin. Listen to what the quiet ones in the congregation are saying. Listen to what is not being said. Listen to what you yourself are saying and the impression you are giving others. Be careful in your conversation and do not demean women, not because women are too sensitive, but because women are too valuable to the Kingdom of God.

Nowhere in this book has this writer indicated that she is objective on this subject. There is only one side of this issue and that is egalitarian. Equal—no buts.

CHAPTER 21

Women will have to decide

Few women want to be deacons or pastors. But when you deny that privilege to any one woman, you have denied it to every woman in your church. You have told every woman that her husband and any other male member of her family, and all those men inside the church where she worships, are superior to her. By your actions, you have told your daughter that her brother is superior to her.

Stop and think about this, because this is what you are saying by your actions. Is this really how you feel? If you do not feel that your sons are better than your daughters, then it is time to step up and say so. Husbands, if you do not feel that you, along with all the boys and men in your church, are superior to your wives, then it is time for you to stand up and say so.

Women, will you be the voices for our daughters and granddaughters? Daughters need our voices. Young women today have never been denied the right to vote or serve on a jury. They have not been denied a credit card based on their gender. They do not know of a time when married women could not purchase a car or buy a house in their own name, simply because they were married and married women were not allowed to enter into certain contractual agreements. *Young women today do not remember a time before 1964 that if they were married, their husbands had to sign for them to buy or sell property, even if it was an inheritance from their own family.*

Many young women in Texas do not know that it wasn't until 1972 that a married woman attorney could sign a client's bond, and married women physicians actually had the right by law to perform various procedures required by their medical practices. They do not remember when women were limited to certain jobs and certain fields of education. In contrast to those times, women can now be educated in any field they choose, and they have legal rights to practice their profession under the law.[1]

Churches deny capable spiritual women equality

Women still do not have full Constitutional equality with men, but, in 1964, the Civil Rights Act gave all women, both black and white, many of the same rights that men already had. The church should have been the first! But they did not stand up for full equality for women in the secular world then, and most will not stand up for women in the church now.

Churches have continually denied capable spiritual women equality before God within their congregations. Women are denied equality by an inaccurate interpretation of the Scriptures, by the Baptist Faith and Message 2000, and by the Danvers Statement. Women are denied equality by seminaries that teach male headship. Women are denied ministry equality by many denominations that teach only males can be the pastors, preachers, or priests. And, most shameful of all, women are denied by other women in their congregations who prevent them from pastoring churches and from becoming deacons.

It is imperative that concerned Christians speak out for women because the seminaries that do train women for ministry cannot force churches to hire them. They can teach and bestow theological degrees upon women, but until local churches are willing to hire women as pastors and ministerial staff, these seminary trained women will not experience freedom to follow God's call. And even though they would be advocating for their own employment, these women cannot speak out because what little chance they have of serving a congregation would be diminished if they are seen as being activists.

Those of us who attend church on Sundays, who vote on the by-laws that limit women, must take action and insist that women and men be given equal treatment in our churches.

The Bible does not cast men and women in play-acting roles

Do not be fooled. The Bible does not give men and women roles to play. It is a moral problem of churches when they deny women equality because they did not check out the accuracy of their translations. To make a lasting change for women, the hearts and minds of the people sitting in the pews must be open to equality. How long will God accept the excuse, "But this is what my Bible (translation) says?"

As believers in Christ, everyone has the responsibility to discern for herself or himself if male headship makes sense. Upon close examination of the teachings of Jesus, they will realize that male headship is a false theology.

Because women are told they cannot have authority over men, they are limited by man in answering God's call. It is not God that limits women in service, it is churches. The Baptist Faith and Message 2000 was drafted by some of the same people who drafted the Danvers Statement, and the message is the same. Even though the BF&M 2000 does not specifically say women cannot be deacons, if a Southern Baptist Convention affiliated church endorses the BF&M 2000, and the majority of them do, that church will not allow women deacons.

Women denied ordination in their church

In Baptist churches, and some other evangelical churches, being a deacon or elder is the highest volunteer position non-clergy can hold. In Baptist churches, deacons are ordained, but are not recognized as clergy. Deacons typically attend monthly planning meetings, serve the Lord's Supper, and take up the offering collection. They do not preach, and probably do not even teach a Sunday school class, and there is no obligation to attend church regularly. In most Baptist churches, deacons are chosen using the same qualifications as that of a pastor that is found in 1 Timothy 3.

Education, training, and spiritual gifts are not qualifying factors, nor is marriage, since unmarried men are often chosen and ordained as deacons. The first and foremost qualifying factor is they must be males. Anything else is secondary.

One Baptist pastor said that some churches already have women serving as deacons, but they don't call them deacons. Those churches are in an illicit relationship. It is comparable to dating a woman with no intention of getting married because you have a contract (the church by-laws) that specifically says that you cannot marry *any* woman. Those churches are not being truthful with the congregation, and they are not being truthful with those women. That pastor recognized that the hard part was getting church members to accept the *title of deacon* for women, but unless they make an effort to legitimize women's service, they will continue in this dishonest relationship.

Holding on to the law

The apostle Paul says: "It is for freedom that Christ has set us free" (Galatians 5:1). Paul says there is no freedom in the law, because if one law is demanded, the whole law must be demanded.

Nobody wants to go back to the whole law. So why are there laws that restrict women from serving God equally? These restrictions against women were borne out of a culture that was dominated by males, but now male leadership teaching gives these restrictions the power of law. There are no restrictions against men based upon their gender, and if we believe and teach that Christ fulfilled the law for his church, there can be no restrictive law forbidding women from serving Christ fully as they are gifted. Or, to be accurate, they should be allowed to serve Christ fully, even if they are not qualified, gifted, or otherwise suited for the job – just as men who are not qualified or gifted hold positions in church leadership.

Jesus had harsh words for Pharisees who imposed their strict law on others: "They tie up heavy loads and put them on men's shoulders, but they themselves are not willing to lift a finger to move them."

Yet in spite of Jesus' words, people write books, blog, and preach sermons about the extent to which a woman is required to submit to her husband. Those who desire to restrict women from full service love nothing more than to go into the marketplace and insist that women must not be allowed to have complete freedom in Christ.

None of this is necessary, and none of it is biblical. The Bible does not lay out submission rules for women. This is a heavy load that has been placed on women's shoulders, and also on men's shoulders. Pastors and theologians have made their law more important than people and more important than God's word, and these makers of the law do not even agree among themselves.

Jesus said: "Take my yoke upon you and learn from me, for I am gentle and humble in heart, and you shall find rest for your souls. For my yoke is easy and my burden (*lack of burdensome and restrictive rules*) is light."

Women must decide to be heirs according to the promise

It cannot be said strongly enough, when churches deny any woman the freedom to be a pastor, a deacon, or an elder, then every woman in that congregation has been denied. When women refuse to allow other women the freedom to serve as pastors, deacons, or elders, they are denying equality for themselves. The greater problem when women refuse to accept the equality they were given at creation is that they are abdicating their own responsibility to serve.

Jocelyn Andersen says in *Woman, this is WAR!* "It is safe to say that no single group of people has suffered consistently, from the dawn of history, from social, political, and religious prejudice more than women." She goes on to say that the Bible teaches that in the beginning both male and female were equal, but according to our history books, there was never a time in all of history, saving the present in some countries, when females were considered autonomous human beings on social and political par with males." She says Paul was seeking to remedy inequality with the Christians in Galatia when he tried to break down the greatest of walls, the one between males and females, when he restored women to their original equality with men. "There is neither Jew nor Greek, slave nor free, male nor female, for you are all one in Christ Jesus. If you belong to Christ, then you are Abraham's seed, and heirs according to the promise." (Galatians 3:28-29).

At some point women will have to decide. There are two choices: women can claim full equality as heirs according to the promise (Galatians 3:29); or they can be children of Hagar the bondwoman (Galatians 4:30-31).

Women must make a commitment for gender equality

Why should pastors speak out and jeopardize their careers if women in their congregations earnestly believe they are commanded by God to let their husbands and other males have authority over them in church and in the home? Why should denominational leaders speak out for equality when most of their peers do not believe women are equal?

This is why they should speak out: because it is a sin to teach that women are inferior in God's kingdom.

Churches are in sin when they classify male human beings as superior to female human beings. God did not do that. Humans have done that. Humans have made males the standard and have decreed that those who are not males are inferior. Men and women have decided this is God's will.

What can we do?

There are things that both women and men can do to make a difference and to advocate for gender equality. First of all, follow the Commit to 5 plan. This is a plan that anybody can do, and it can be started at any time. Involve your Sunday school class, your Bible study group, or individually commit to one or more of the five suggested ways to further women's equality. Choose from the list and commit to five months to learn more about women's equality. Your life will be changed.

Commit to 5 for individuals and groups

- Pray daily for women's equality (also known as gender equality or gender inclusivity).
- Learn more about women's equality by reading at least one article and one book that promotes gender equality (a good resource is www.cbeinternational.org).
- Attend a small group Bible study or book discussion group, facebook, or internet group that promotes women's equality.
- Make one change in the way you speak about women's equality among your church small group or Bible study class, or in how you participate in worship services and church activities.
- Share your journey with at least one other person who you think will be blessed with the knowledge of women's equality.

Make it personal

Women, tell your pastors how degraded it makes you feel when you walk into your church with the knowledge that your church does not see you as a full church member with all the rights and responsibilities afforded the men.

Men, tell your pastors that after studying scripture, you find it unacceptable for your church to tell your wife or your daughters they are not as valuable as you are in service of your church. Tell your pastors that they know scripture, and they know how Jesus elevated women, not through flattery, but with the heart of the gospel, expecting women to go and tell. Men, tell your pastors that your church should do no less.

Let your pastors know that you want women to be able to walk into church and feel that your church values them as complete in the sight of God, and not just as a *complement* to their husbands. Your church will tell you that they do value women, and will say the words women hear over and over, "We couldn't run the church without the women."

They mean only half of it. They mean that it is mainly women who bring the kids to church, who teach the kids, and who work tirelessly.

What they fail to mention is that it is only men who preach and serve as deacons, who are permitted to pray out loud, or read scriptures to the congregation, and whose membership comes without physical restrictions.

Learn from others who are working for equality

Connect with those working for women's equality. Christians for Biblical Equality (www.cbeinternational.org) is in the forefront of speaking out and promoting women's equality. There are chapters in several states which provide opportunity to network with like-minded egalitarian Christians. CBE provides literature, teaching and speaking helps, and conferences devoted to teaching biblical equality of women.

Encourage your daughters and sons to attend seminaries that support women in ministry. Find out what they teach before any money is spent.

It is a testimony to their love of God that women go to church at all considering the way they are demeaned in most churches. A church's legal documents tell women what they cannot do. Instead of worrying about the so-called feminization of the church, denominational church leaders should be concerned about the rejection and lack of love shown toward women in the church.

Women are tired of hearing sermons about their responsibility in marriage without full accountability being demanded from their husbands. Women want to walk into their churches and not feel that their church holds it against them that they are women. Women want their daughters to have the same opportunities as their sons have to serve God. Young girls are hearing a call of service from God but are being denied that call by their churches.

Church membership for women and men is unequal

When a man and a woman stand before a complementarian church to be accepted into membership, the man is welcomed into full membership of the church while the woman is accepted with restrictions placed upon her membership, some of which are written in the by-laws. These restrictions may not all be written down but are commonly understood, and in many cases the restrictions depend upon what the individual congregation has decided. As a woman, she cannot be considered for certain positions within the church for one reason only—her physical anatomy.

The church determines how women will be considered in the home. Complementarian teaching is that men lead women in the church and in the home. Egalitarian teaching says both men and women are leaders who are equal in both home and church. It is spiritual gifts—not gender—that determines how women and men are to fit into the work of the church.

The purpose of this book is not to belittle men, feminize men, or emasculate men. Men are precious in God's kingdom, in the family, and in the church. Women are equally precious in God's kingdom, in the family, and in the church.

Scripture has already dethroned male headship. Now it is up to us.

CHAPTER 22

Egalitarian Resistance Movement

Much to the surprise of the Council on Biblical Manhood and Womanhood, egalitarians are not giving up.

The Danvers Statement that was the charter statement of the CBMW was conceived in 1984 and written in 1987 and is the largest single influence of male headship since women have gotten the right to vote. Before the 1920s, women were hampered by legal restrictions, lack of education, limited mobility, pregnancy and large families, and restrictive clothing. Sixty years after the vote, men were again binding women to restrictive leadership roles in the church and home.

Wayne Grudem surprised at the resistance

Restrictions against women in church leadership can be laid directly at the feet of Wayne Grudem, professor of theology and biblical studies, who penned the premise of the Danvers Statement and called for the first meetings which founded the Council on Biblical Manhood and Womanhood. While Grudem says that he is coming to the end of his advocacy for male headship (female submission), his work lives on in an increasingly larger way through others who received the mantle.

It did not turn out the way Grudem thought. There is a resistance that he did not expect, and while CBMW's determination remains strong and their actions are more visible, there is a movement for equality as both women and men are calling for the end to male headship.

In Grudem's own words:

"I am surprised that this controversy has gone on so long. In the late 80s and early 90s when we began this, I expected that this would probably be over in ten years. By force of argument, by use of facts, by careful exegesis, by the power of the clear word of God, by the truth, I expected the entire church would be persuaded, the battle for the purity of the church would be won, and egalitarian advocates would be marginalized and have no significant influence. But it has not completely happened yet!

"I still believe it will happen. Jesus Christ is building and purifying his church that he might present it to himself without spot or wrinkle. But on this issue Christ's purification process is taking much longer than I expected!"[1] (CBMW Journal April 2012)

As a professor of theology and biblical studies, Grudem would know that just because someone claims that God is directing and leading, does not make it true. In fact, the Danvers Statement Affirmation #8 spells it out, "In both men and women, a heartfelt sense of call to the ministry should never be used to set aside biblical criteria for particular ministries. Rather, biblical teaching should remain the authority for testing our subjective discernment of God's will."

Therefore, Grudem feels one thing, while others see God's working in a different direction, based upon a different interpretation of biblical teaching.

Additionally, it is extremely offensive when Grudem makes the comment that the purification of the church includes wiping out women in leadership roles in the church and also in their own homes.

The larger question is: how can pastors and husbands read Grudem's words and not find complete revulsion in the arrogance of purifying the church of women?

Egalitarian Resistance Movement

There are many groups, organizations, and individuals working for women's equality in the church. Some are connected to particular denominations such as Baptist Women in Ministry (Southern Baptists); Women Priests (Roman Catholics), I Support Women's Ordination in Adventism (Seventh Day Adventists), Ordain Women Now (Lutheran Missouri Synod), Ordain Women (Mormons).

At some point, there will have to be a tipping factor. We can't balance the seesaw forever. Either we make the break and head for victory, or our voices will be silenced for a very long time. It is up to those who care that the gospel of Jesus Christ is preached by both men and women to make that happen.

Christians for Biblical Equality

Christians for Biblical Equality[2] (CBE) and the Council on Biblical Manhood and Womanhood (CBMW) were birthed in the same timeframe of 1987-1988, and on completely opposite sides of the equality controversy. CBE is headquartered in Minneapolis, Minnesota, near Bethel College in St. Paul, Minnesota, where CBMW's Wayne Grudem was a professor, and is close to CMBW's John Piper's Bethlehem Church. This connection is important to understand, because it is these two groups who are the strongest advocates of their respective positions.

Just as CBMW has its notable names, CBE does, too. Gilbert Bilezikian, Stanley Gundry, Gretchen Gaebelein Hull, and Catherine Clark Kroeger, the first president of CBE, have become household names to those working for equality.

CBE believes that the overarching principle of the Bible is that men and women are equally created in God's image; equally responsible for sin; equally redeemed by Christ; equally gifted by God's Spirit for service; and equally held responsible for using their God-given gifts.

Their website is a great source for egalitarian books and articles on gender equality. They publish their scholarly journal *Pricilla Papers*, and their ministry magazine *Mutuality*, and the free enewsletter *Arise*. They publish egalitarian curriculum for youth in several languages.

Membership is open to churches, seminaries, universities, organizations and individuals. CBE is international and holds their yearly conferences in the United States one year and the next year the conference is held in a different country. CBE has grown to include members from over 100 denominations and 65 countries. Contact www.cbeinternational.org.

Equity for Women in the Church

There is a new kid on the block and she is called "Equity for Women in the Church."[3] Birthed as a community in the Alliance of Baptists in 2013, and formalized in 2015, Equity for Women in the Church is comprised of clergy, denominational, and seminary leaders across the country from various races, genders, and 10 denominations.

Rev. Jann Aldredge-Clanton pointed out that "since recent religious history shows that 2 or 3 committed people (such as what Paige Patterson and Paul Pressler did with the Southern Baptist Convention) meeting and planning can take over a denomination and move it backwards to exclude women called to ministry, surely 30 committed people meeting and planning can move denominations forward to open doors for women called to pastor churches. These Equity for Women in the Church Activists intend to do just that!" Contact www.equityforwomeninthechurch.org.

They are currently focusing on three projects:

Calling in the Key of She. Calling in the Key of She is an ecumenical leadership empowerment program for clergy and religious leaders that seeks to address the gap of female leadership in Protestant churches by educating and empowering congregations to become more "female-friendly." This also includes programs to impact adolescent girls and boys at an early age by educating them, exposing them to female clergy and religious leaders, and allowing them to explore various aspects of ministry available to all persons.

Retiring Pastors Initiative. This project enlists senior/solo pastors who may retire in the next 3-5 years to prepare their congregations to consider women pastoral candidates. A survey will identify pastors who are willing to use specific strategies to break down barriers that may hinder a congregation from considering and calling the best candidate irrespective of gender. Retiring pastor participants will receive resources such as books, videos, consultation, and online support.

The Lydia Project. This project will provide financial support to clergywomen who create new and renewed multicultural, welcoming and affirming Christian communities who practice inclusivity in language, gender, and race. Equity will partner with seminaries/theological schools in selecting clergywomen to support.

We will not be marginalized

It is time to stand up. It is time to speak up against this atrocity against women and against the gospel of Jesus Christ.

We are the egalitarian resistance movement and we will not be marginalized!

Conclusion

Over fifty years ago when my husband Don and I got married, churches did not dwell on women submitting to their husbands. It was accepted that men were the head of the household because men made more money than women, so it was up to them to support the family. Leadership was not mentioned, and many families understood that their mothers were actually the leaders in the family, both in the spiritual realm and the secular.

The natural progression, as we moved forward in the 20th century, would have been for churches to accept women in church leadership just as women were being accepted to colleges and places of business. In fact, the church should have been the first to raise women up in status. But they did not do that. Instead, churches reacted with vehemence against women. They wanted to hold on to the male feel of Christianity, and they did.

But as in everything, too much power is destructive. They have set a course of male headship and female submission that is detrimental to Christianity.

The words of freedom

Women in Paul's day were adversely affected by this same kind of power. Paul knew this. Read Ephesians 5:25-29 with fresh eyes and listen to what Paul was really saying. He started with the ideal marriage in verse 25: "…husbands, love your wives, as Christ loved the church." He knew that many husbands abused their wives, so he had to get the marriage situation straight because Christ is not abusive. So he said that husbands should love their wives as their own bodies (verse 28). That meant only one thing to those women. They heard Paul saying "Husbands, treat your wives just like you would treat yourself, your own body. Do not beat your wife. You would not give yourself a black eye, so do not give her one."

How these women must have rejoiced in this new-found Christian living!

The words of freedom that caused Christian women of the early church to rejoice are the same words used today to keep Christians bound to a first century culture. They are the same words that many use today to emotionally coerce women into unbiblical obedience to their husbands.

Complementarians have picked out certain scriptures from the Bible that they feel reinforce their teaching of female submission and male authority even though the overall theme of the Gospel is that women are equal in salvation, service, and responsibility.

The Bible was used as an argument for slavery at one time. And, just as owning another human being is now recognized as being evil, someday we will recognize that men claiming authority over women is not what the Bible teaches. Having authority over women puts husbands on par with divinity, and we know that man is not divine.

Churches stubbornly cling to pet doctrines about male superiority that are nothing more than links to the past that still bind women in the 21st century. Pastors like to think of themselves as being modern, so 21st century, but when they deny Christian women equality, they are promoting a culture that is outdated and antiquated, and *which has no biblical basis for continuation*. They fail to see that they have fallen into the same bias against women that has restricted women for centuries. Women themselves do not realize these restrictions are remnant rags from a previous culture that are clinging to them.

We burden men and women with the yoke of submission

American soldiers have been fighting in Afghanistan and Iraq since 2001. These are countries where culture and religion keep women subjugated to men. By law in these countries, women must be silent and unseen in public. Our American soldiers, both men and women, find themselves fighting for Afghan women's rights. The irony is that when they come home, these men soldiers will likely be told in their churches that they have authority over their own wives. They will be told their wives must submit to them. The returning women soldiers will be told that they must submit to their husbands, similar to what the women in Afghanistan are required to do. Remember, for those who accept complementarianism, it is always up to the husband to determine to what degree he demands submission from his wife.

Christians are missionary people who send men and women to foreign countries to spread the gospel. In many of these countries missionaries find women who are mistreated by their husbands and by the government. Women are mutilated by a circumcision process, are sex-trafficked, and many women live in homes with husbands who have multiple wives. Their customs demand that they obey their husbands. Often they live in deplorable conditions. We give them the message of hope through Jesus Christ. Then, we turn around and burden them down again with the yoke of submission, ignoring Paul's words in Galatians 5: "It is for freedom that Christ has set us free. Stand firm, then, and do not let yourselves be burdened again by a yoke of slavery."

We have a dark secret that is kept at home.

We, too, keep women in submission.

How did the church go so terribly wrong?

Look to the seminaries for the answer to where the church went wrong. Especially look to those seminaries of the founding members or later members of the Council on Biblical Manhood and Womanhood, who devised the Danvers Statement, and composed the Baptist Faith and Message 2000. Only a few of the members have been mentioned in this book, and at the time of this writing, still hold these positions:

- Paige Patterson, president of Southwestern Baptist Theological Seminary
- Dorothy Patterson, adjunct faculty, Southwestern Baptist Theological Seminary (wife of Paige Patterson)

- Wayne Grudem, professor of Bible and Theology, Phoenix Seminary
- Mary Kassian, professor of Women's Studies, Southern Baptist Theological Seminary
- George W Knight, adjunct professor, Greenville Presbyterian Theological Seminary
- Bruce Ware, professor of Christian Theology, Southern Baptist Theological Seminary

Not mentioned elsewhere in this book is Chuck Kelley, President of New Orleans Baptist Theological Seminary, who helped write the Baptist Faith and Message 2000 and who is the brother of Dorothy Patterson. Kelley's wife, Rhonda Kelley, is the director of Women's Academic Programs at New Orleans Baptist Theological Seminary and is professor of Women's Ministry at NOBTS's Leavell College, which is the college for their undergraduate program.

Complementarianism and the Baptist Faith & Message 2000 is all in the family. Of the 55 SBC seminaries and satellite campuses, the Patterson and Kelley families preside over 26 of those. Their complementarian influence is far-reaching. And do not think for a minute it is just Baptists that are affected. *Many* other denominations secure pastors and youth ministers from these seminaries. That is one reason complementarianism and the BF&M 2000 has successfully transcended denominational lines.

Southwestern Baptist Theological Seminary teaches women homemaking courses. Seminaries are supposed to teach theology! But they do this because SBC seminaries claim homemaking is women's place as set forth in the Danvers Statement and by the Baptist Faith and Message 2000. That is to be expected since Dorothy Patterson, who is on the adjunct faculty at Southwestern Baptist Theological Seminary, is listed first as 'homemaker' on the website of the Council on Biblical Manhood and Womanhood, as are the other women. That is ridiculous.

Southeastern Baptist Theological Seminary allows women to earn a Master of Divinity degree with the notation "with women's studies," which gives them a degree with restrictions. This school does not recognize the Holy Spirit's gifting to women. Southeastern Seminary boasts "The concentration provided by this track will prepare women for a wide variety of family, care-giving, and mission ministries." But women cannot teach men.

Degrees earned by female graduates of these institutions always come with restrictions, and women will continually be discriminated against by seminaries that teach male leadership over women unless action is taken against it.

Jesus had strong words of rebuke for the teachers of the law

Jesus had strong words of rebuke for the teachers of the law who loved their law more than they loved the people who were hindered by their strict interpretation of that law. They gave their required tithe and thought that gave them the right to do as they pleased. So when it came to treating people with compassion, they failed. Jesus said this failing outweighed their keeping of the law (Matthew 23:23). Amos 5:21-24 says the same thing, paraphrased: "Your religious activities, your songs, and your money do not mean a thing to me. What I am concerned about is that you are not showing justice to others."

Some seminary professors and pastors are guilty of this lack of justice toward the largest segment of humanity—women. There is a constant barrage of self-righteous indignation against women who hear the call to preach. Complementarian bloggers love nothing more than to criticize women's equality and argue whether or not women have scriptural permission to do anything in church, except teach other women and children.

One-fifth of Americans have no religious affiliation, but the concern is not to provide a preacher for those lost souls, instead the concern is that some *woman* might feel called to preach to them, or feel called to be a deacon or elder, or to fill a position where she might exercise some spiritual authority over a man.

Like those Jesus chastised, the bad behavior of many legalistic complementarian leaders outweighs any good they might do. Teachers and preachers should take note of what Jesus said. Teachers of the law have it wrong again.

Can husbands accept judgment in their wives' place?

Complementarian pastors sometimes teach that husbands will stand accountable before God for their wives at the judgment day. It is likely they learned that in a Southern Baptist Convention affiliated seminary. As shown in Chapter 12, "What the Danvers Statement REALLY means," Dorothy Patterson was quoted as saying, "As a woman standing under the authority of Scripture, even when it comes to submitting to my husband when I know he's wrong, I just have to do it, and then he stands accountable at the judgment."[1] That statement makes her husband "Christ" for her because she believes he takes her sins upon himself, and accepts judgment in her place.

Most have never heard of the Danvers Statement

In 2009 when I first began my ministry of working for women's equality, I had never heard of the Danvers Statement or the Council on Biblical Manhood and Womanhood. Even though I had worked for Baptist General Convention of Texas for almost 15 years, I had no idea CBMW was behind the new Baptist Faith and Message 2000, and that their founding members were presidents and professors at Southern Baptist Theological seminaries. Just as I was uninformed, most Baptists today are woefully ignorant regarding the lack of women's equality in their congregation.

In fact, a member of a Baptist megachurch recently asked me if Baptists allow women ministers. His church does not have Baptist in the name and he did not know that the church he attends each Sunday with his family is, in fact, Baptist. He said he thought women should be pastors. There are many men and women sitting in Baptist pews who would welcome women pastors. It is my prayer that someday soon, they will find their voices and speak up for women's equality. It is also my prayer that they will find help in this book to bring this about.

The seminary presidents and professors mentioned in this book are past retirement age, but they are still in place and still training those who will follow. They have created an empire of discrimination against women and have found many who choose to follow. It is hoped that love and justice and reevaluation of what Jesus came to tell us, will upend this empire that chooses to "Lord it over" women.

They are still learning at the feet of those who crafted the Danvers Statement

The words of this book are not intended to be an indictment against men, but the *words* of this book *are* intended to be an indictment against the *false teaching* that God made men superior to women.

Those who wonder why anyone would bring up the Danvers Statement on Biblical Manhood and Womanhood because it is almost 30 years old, needs to be reminded that it is still the driving force behind complementarian teaching today. Many young preachers in seminary today are still learning at the feet of those who crafted it.

10 questions
Christians should answer

1. Why are Christians afraid of equality between men and women?
2. What damage is it doing to young girls and women in the church today who feel the calling of God on their lives?
3. What will it do to young men if they believe they will have authority over women when they grow up?
4. Where did the evil phrase *feminization of the church* come from that causes unjustified fear that men will quit going to church if women become pastors?
5. How do Christians justify allowing women to have authority over children and youth, who are more susceptible to false teaching, when women cannot have authority over men who are supposedly wiser and less likely to be wrongly influenced?
6. Are Christians afraid of losing particular denominational beliefs—what will it do to denominational identities if churches do change, and does it matter in the long run?
7. How are those Christian churches viewed that have taken the step of having women as pastors?
8. How does it make women feel when they are told from the pulpit that they are to submit to their husbands in all things? How does it make men feel?
9. What will be accomplished by continuing this rejection of women as pastors and deacons?
10. How will Christians answer God when He asks the church why they did not use the people He called?

Notes

Introduction

1. Danvers Statement on Biblical Manhood and Womanhood.
http://swbts.edu/about/affirmed-statements/the-danvers-statement/
2. Baptist Faith and Message 2000.
http://www.sbc.net/bfm2000/bfm2000.asp.

Chapter 1. In the Beginning

1. Giles, Kevin. The Eternal Subordination of the Son of God and the Perma-nent Subordination of Women. Giles is the author of The Trinity and Subor-dinationism: The Doctrine of God and the Contemporary Gender Debate (InterVarsity, 2002) and Jesus and the Father: Modern Evangelicals Reinvent the Doctrine of the Trinity. http://www.catalystresources.org/the-eternal-subordination-of-the-son-of-god-and-the-permanent-subordination-of-women/.
2. Grudem, Wayne. Biblical Foundations for Manhood and Womanhood. 2002 Crossway Books, pp 25-37. Additionally, Ten Reasons for Male Headship. Grudem gives 10 reasons why male headship was established before the fall, Todd Murray, March 23, 2011.
http://www.bclrblog.org/2011/03/ten-reasons-for-male-headship.html.
3. Andersen, Jocelyn. *Woman This is WAR! Gender, Slavery and the Evangelical Caste System.* One Way Press, pub 2010. Pages 212-213.

Chapter 2. They asked for Sarah first

1. Ware, Bruce. The Father, the Son, and the Holy Spirit: The Trinity as Theo-logical Foundation for Family Ministry. "I find it astonishing that it is in this text, of all New Testament passages that teach on husband and wife relations, that the strongest language is used to describe a wife's submission! Peter ap-pealed to Sarah as an example and said that she "obeyed Abraham, calling him lord" (1 Pet 3:6a), indicating that they would be Sarah's "children" if they fear-lessly followed this example (1 Pet 3:6b) (5)." Implications for Mothers and Fa-

thers.   http://www.sbts.edu/family/2011/10/10/the-father-the-son-and-the-holy-spirit-the-trinity-as-theological-foundation-for-family-ministry/.

Chapter 8. God does not share headship with man

1. Allen, Bob. Video of women's rights meeting posted online, October 10, 2010. Doug Phillips was a speaker at the Seneca Falls 2 Christian Women's Right Convention in Orlando, Florida, July 24, 2010.

Chapter 12. What the Danvers Statement REALLY says

1. Grudem, Wayne. Personal reflections on the history of CBMW and the state of the gender debate. http://cbmw.org/uncategorized/personal-reflections-on-the-history-of-cbmw-and-the-state-of-the-gender-debate/

2. The Danvers Statement on Biblical Manhood and Womanhood. http://swbts.edu/about/affirmed-statements/the-danvers-statement/.

3. Egalitarianism and homosexuality http://cbmw.org/ uncategorized/egalitarianism-and-homosexuality/

4. Allen, Bob. Professor's Views on Spouse Abuse Don't Square With SBC Statements. http://www.ethicsdaily.com/professors-views-on-spouse-abuse-dont-square-with-sbc-statements-cms-12968.

Chapter 13. Apology Demand

1. Allen, Bob, ABPNews.com. Christians demand apology for anti-woman teaching.   http://www.abpnews.com/archives/item/5370-christians-demand-apology-for-anti-women-teaching.

Chapter 14. What male headship means

1. Kaniaru,Vicky and Miller, Norm. College faculty inks Baptist Faith and Message. http://www.bpnews.net/bpnews.asp?id=36449.

2. Allen, Bob. Professor's Views on Spouse Abuse Don't Square With SBC Statements. http://www.ethicsdaily.com/professors-views-on-spouse-abuse-dont-square-with-sbc-statements-cms-12968.

Chapter 15. Male headship distorts marriage

1. Allen, Bob. Professor's Views on Spouse Abuse Don't Square With SBC Statements.

http://www.ethicsdaily.com/professors-views-on-spouse-abuse-dont-square-with-sbc-statements-cms-12968.

2. CNA Catholic News Agency. Marriage is the instrument of salvation for all of society declares Benedict XVI.

http://www.catholicnewsagency.com/news/marriage_is_instrument_of_salvation_for_all_of_society_declares_benedict_xvi/.

3. Piper, John. Does a woman submit to abuse?

www.youtube.com/watch?feature=player_embedded&v=3OkUPc2NLrM.

4. Piper, John. Piper's Notes MARRIAGE: A MATRIX OF CHRISTIAN HEDONISM. Ephesians 5:21-33, October 16, 1983.

http://www.pipersnotes.com/piper83/101683m.htm.

5. Ware, Bruce. Revive Our Hearts. Interview with Nancy Leigh DeMoss. Men and women in the church.

https://www.reviveourhearts.com/radio/revive-our-hearts/men-and-women-in-the-church/

6. Scriptures mentioning the Bride.

http://www.openbible.info/topics/the_bride_of_christ

Chapter 17. Eternal Son Subordination flawed theology

1. Giles, Kevin. The Eternal Subordination of the Son of God and the Permanent Subordination of Women. Giles is the author of *The Trinity and* Subordinationism: *The Doctrine of God and the Contemporary Gender Debate* (InterVarsity, 2002) and *Jesus and the Father: Modern Evangelicals Reinvent the Doctrine of the Trinity.*

http://www.catalystresources.org/the-eternal-subordination-of-the-son-of-god-and-the-permanent-subordination-of-women/.

2. Kunsman, Cynthia RN, BSN, ND, MMin. www.undermuchgrace.com.

3. Ware, Bruce. The Father, the Son, and the Holy Spirit: The Trinity as Theological Foundation for Family Ministry. Implications for Husbands and Fathers.

http://www.sbts.edu/family/2011/10/10/the-father-the-son-and-the-holy-spirit-the-trinity-as-theological-foundation-for-family-ministry.

4. Kassian, Mary. Complementarianism for dummies.

http://www.girlsgonewise.com/complementarianism-for-dummies.

5. *The Malleus Maleficarum of Heinrich Kramer and James Sprenger Translated with an Introduction, Bibliography & Notes by the Reverend Montague Summers.* Available in .pdf through several websites.

6. Andersen, Jocelyn. *Woman This is WAR! Gender, Slavery and the Evangelical Caste System.* One Way Press, published 2010.

7. Stanley, Charles. *A Man's Touch.* Victor Books, Wheaton, IL, 1988.

8. Wade Burleson. Eternal Subordination and SBC Divorce Rate.

http://www.wadeburleson.org/2015/06/eternal-subordination-and-sbc-divorce.html

Chapter 18. Sexualizing the Trinity

1. Piper, John. Piper's Notes MARRIAGE: A MATRIX OF CHRISTIAN HEDONISM. Ephesians 5:21-33, October 16, 1983.

http://www.pipersnotes.com/piper83/101683m.htm.

2. Keller, Timothy and Grace. *The Meaning of Marriage. Facing the Complexities of Commitment with the Wisdom of God.* (The Glory of Sex). Penguin Group, pub. 2011.

3. Piper, John & Grudem, Wayne, eds. Recovering Biblical Manhood and Womanhood : A Response to Evangelical Feminism, Edited by John Piper and Wayne Grudem, Crossway Books Wheaton, Illinois, 1991.

4. Kassian, Mary. More Necessities for God Glorifying Sex. Rachel's Questions, "What makes complementarian sex different from egalitarian sex?" Oct.18, 2012.

http://www.girlsgonewise.com/more-necessities-for-god-glorifying-sex/.

5. Kassian, Mary. More Necessities for God Glorifying Sex. Rachel's Questions, "What does it mean to carry male-female roles over into the marriage bed?" October 18, 2012.

http://www.girlsgonewise.com/more-necessities-for-god-glorifying-sex/.

6. Kumar, Anugrah, Christian Post Contributor, January 15, 2012. 'Sexperiment:' Ed Young Suffers Eye Injury; Leaves Before 24 Hours Over.

http://www.christianpost.com/news/sexperiment-ed-young-suffers-eye-injury-leaves-before-24-hours-over-67182/#JJbTTWmsLUOkVdYq.99.

7. Pastor Darren Walter, Sex is God's idea. http://www.ibtimes.com/texas-pastor-gives-popular-sex-sermons-ahead-valentines-day-1807910

8. Mark Driscoll returns to evangelical orbit. http://blog.seattlepi.com/seattlepolitics/2015/03/12/ex-mars-hill-pastor-mark-driscoll-returns-to-evangelical-orbit/

9. Mark Driscoll ministries makes a comeback. http://www.patheos.com/blogs/warrenthrockmorton/2015/04/01/mark-driscolls-website-gets-a-makeover-learning-for-living-becomes-mark-driscoll-ministries/.

10. Driscoll, Mark and Grace. *Real Marriage. The Truth about Sex, Friendship and Life Together.* Thomas Nelson, pub. 2012.

11. Burk, Denny. (Staff journal writer for Council on Biblical Manhood and Womanhood). My Review of Mark Driscoll's *Real Marriage.* The Can We ____? Chapter and Direct Revelations from God http://www.dennyburk.com/my-review-of-mark-driscolls-real-marriage/.

12. Driscoll, Mark. Tough Text Tuesday: 1Timothy 2:15. Note: Mark Driscoll has returned to ministry and has created a new website which does not carry his old sermons and notes. Before his resignation from Mars Hill Church, this was posted: http://pastormark.tv/2011/10/25/tough-text-tuesday-1-timothy-2-15.

Chapter 19. How churches teach male headship

1. Revive Our Hearts. Interview with Nancy Leigh DeMoss. https://www.reviveourhearts.com/radio/revive-our-hearts/men-and-women-in-the-church/

2. Mathis, David. More on the Masculine Feel of Christianity. http://www.desiringgod.org/blog/posts/more-on-the-masculine-feel-of-christianity.

3. Grudem, Wayne. Which Church Roles Should Be Open to Women. http://www.beliefnet.com/Faiths/Christianity/2006/11/Which-Church-Roles-Should-Be-Open-To-Women.aspx?p=1.

4. John Piper. Recovering Biblical Manhood and Womanhood: A Response to A Response to Evangelical Feminism. Edited by John Piper and Wayne Grudem. Crossway books, Wheaten, Illinois, A Division of Good News Publishers. Page 48

5. Kassian, Mary. The Gospel Coalition. *Boundaries are for your freedom.* http://vimeo.com/45908532.

Chapter 20. Pastors' responsibility to the whole congregation

1. Big Day Events (that you can host.) http://media.mobaptist.org/public/evangelism/big-day-events/BigDayEvent5.pdf

2. Shoals Creek Outdoors Wild Game Event. (Guest speaker, Paige Patterson, President of Southwestern Baptist Theological Seminary in Fort Worth, Texas). http://shoalcreekchurch.org/events/?eventID=178.

3. Sandra Crawford Williamson. Why are Working Women Starting to Unplug from Their churches? http://blog.tifwe.org/working-women-unplugging-from-church/

Chapter 21. Women will have to decide

1. Enstam, Elizabeth York. Women and the law. http://www.tshaonline.org/handbook/online/articles/jsw02.

Chapter 22. Egalitarian Resistance Movement

1. Grudem, Wayne. Personal reflections on the history of CBMW and the state of the gender debate. http://cbmw.org/uncategorized/personal-reflections-on-the-history-of-cbmw-and-the-state-of-the-gender-debate/

2. Christians for Biblical Equality. www.cbeinternational.org

3. Equity for Women in the Church. http://equityforwomeninthechurch.org/blog/

Conclusion

1. Kennedy, John W. "Patterson's Election Seals Conservative Control," *Christianity Today*, 13 July 1998, 21. http://www.christianitytoday.com/ct/1998/july13/8t8021.html?start=2.

Dethroning Male Headship

What is the book *Dethroning Male Headship* about?

It is about changing the way churches and society view women based upon the Bible. The Bible is being used to keep women in submission to their husbands by something that is called women's "roles." Of course men have "roles" also, but their roles are unlimited while women are denied positions in church that are perceived as giving women authority over men, positions such as a woman being a pastor or being a deacon.

Your book might be considered controversial among Christians.

Oh, yes, it is controversial. The majority of evangelical Christians subscribe to the teaching that men are born having authority over women and that women who claim they are called to be ministers are stepping outside their biblical womanhood roles. Southern Baptists are the largest Protestant group and that is the denomination I am familiar with since I was employed by Texas Baptists for almost 15 years. However, male headship teaching, also called complementarian, is predominant in many faith groups and denominations.

Why do you think your book is relevant now?

It is 2015 and women are still being told every Sunday morning in church that they are inferior to their husbands, citing the Bible as the reason. However, the Bible does not teach submission as a biblical commandment for the future. It is time women claimed their equality and it is time pastors and seminary professors teach that women are created fully equal—no buts.

What harm does it do to practice male headship?

It is a sin against God when his female creation is told that any and all males are designed by God to have authority over her. Churches pretty up the words and say it is just the husband who has authority over his wife; however, when they deny women positions in church because she is female, you see the truth is they believe that *all men* have authority over *all* women *all* of the time.

What makes you think you can make a difference when others have failed?

Our voices lend weight to each other and our voices are becoming louder and will not be stilled.

Shirley Taylor writes with passion

- We have a dark secret that we keep at home. We, too, keep women in submission.
- It is not qualifications nor is it spirituality that makes men desirable as leaders in the church. It is the male body. What is not explained is how this adoration of the male body translates into worship of God.
- Look to the seminaries for the answer to where the church went wrong.
- Remember, it is always up to the husband to determine to what degree he demands submission from his wife.
- When you accept that translation, you have accepted divinity for human males.
- The greater problem when women refuse to accept the equality they were given at creation is that they are abdicating their own responsibility to serve.

Shirley Taylor writes with humor

- If Adam had been a male headship kind of guy, he would have knocked that apple out of Eve's hand and picked up a stick and killed that snake. Alas! Male headship ate the apple.
- His loving, humble headship did not rise to the occasion.
- If that doesn't make you queasy, then I don't know what will!
- If you believe that, then you need to get yourself a real Bible.
- If you do not think that makes a woman feel inferior, then you need to rethink your definition of inferior.

Shirley Taylor writes for action

- It is a testimony to their love of God that women go to church at all considering the way they are demeaned in most churches. A church's legal documents tell women what they cannot do in church.
- Pastors are deciding now if they want to continue to be part of the problem - holding back women's equality - or if they want to follow Christ and be part of the solution.
- At some point, women will have to decide if they want freedom or if they want to be bound by restrictions.

Reviews for
Dethroning Male Headship

In Dethroning Male Headship, Shirley Taylor explains egalitarianism means women and men are created "equal—no buts" and have no pre-assigned "roles of authority or submission" based on gender. [...] Taylor provides numerous scriptural references, including passages not only to specific women but also to the Ten Commandments and the Apostle Paul's teachings.

Kathy Robinson Hillman, First Vice President,
Baptist General Convention of Texas (later President)

Shirley Taylor writes with an insight and clarity that often eludes others with compelling style. She builds each case with plenty of details and references, then the reiteration at the end provides a great summary. While this is a very contentious subject, she has met it head on and provides a convincing argument that scripture has been misinterpreted or even distorted to maintain the status quo and male authority over women.

Sharon Martin

This book is prophetic in its intensity and message. The author names names and groups that contribute to holding down Christian women from being all they can be in Christ and calls on those names and groups to repent. Furthermore, she gives concrete ideas on actions to take to combat this sin in the church today.

Donald Byron Johnson

In an age of declining church membership and influence, human trafficking, pornography and other social ills, it is sinful for the church to focus on male dominance over females. And she makes a powerful case. And throughout the book she makes points that I've never heard anyone make before- but they make a lot of sense! She does it all in an interesting, inspiring style. Dethroning Male Headship is an important addition to the fight for Biblical equality.

Greg Hahn

This is one of the best books I have read in a long time defining the true meaning of headship is vital to Christ centeredness, the oneness of the body and proper spiritual maturity.

An Avid Reader

Shirley's book demonstrates that the only means by which the complementarians really have to run back to Adam comes through legalism, condemnation, manipulation, and control - all while they call it love and God's divine order.

Cynthia Kunsman

Shirley Taylor shows how the husband authority teaching not only distorts marriage, but also makes marriage the instrument of salvation and elevates husbands to being divinity. Unbelievable as it sounds when stated without explanation in a review, this IS what husband-authority preachers are teaching.

Waneta Dawn

ABOUT THE AUTHOR

Shirley Taylor is known locally as the "street evangelist for women's equality." Convinced that Christian women were being held to the confines of the First Century, she founded bWe Baptist Women for Equality to advocate for full equality for Christian women. Shirley is a blogger and has a long history of working for churches. She was employed for over 14 years as a denominational ministry assistant with the Baptist General Convention of Texas. She was a featured speaker at the Seneca Falls 2 Christian Women's Rights Convention held in Orlando, Florida, in 2010. This is her fifth book. She and her husband live in Texas. She loves to hear from readers.

Email her at shirleytaylor777@gmail.com
bWe Baptist Women for Equality
www.shirleytaylor.net

Made in United States
North Haven, CT
30 October 2021